Underwater Guide to
SEYCHELLES

Underwater Guide to
SEYCHELLES

Christophe Mason-Parker & Rowana Walton

JOHN BEAUFOY PUBLISHING

Reprinted in 2022

This edition published in the United Kingdom in 2020 by John Beaufoy Publishing Limited,
11 Blenheim Court, 316 Woodstock Road, Oxford OX2 7NS, U.K.
www.johnbeaufoy.com

10 9 8 7 6 5 4 3 2

ISBN 978-1-912081-27-1

Designed by Gulmohur Press
Project management by Rosemary Wilkinson

Printed and bound in Malaysia by Times Offset (M) Sdn. Bhd.

Photo captions
p.2: Numerous species compete for space on Seychelles' granitic reefs p.3 Teira Batfish (*Platax teira*);
p.5 (top to bottom): Seychelles Anemonefish (*Amphiprion fuscocaudatus*); A
stand of Acropora coral; Coral Hind Grouper (*Cephalopholis miniata*); Nudibranch
(*Hypselodoris pulchella*).

Front cover: Green Turtle. Back cover, top to bottom: Red Emperor Snapper;
Twin Goniobranchus; Schooling Bluelined Snapper

Contents

Introduction to Seychelles

Seychelles is the tropical island paradise that many dream of; its stunning natural beauty both above and below water alongside a rich cultural history and welcoming people, entice thousands of visitors to its shores each year.

Beau Vallon beach, Mahé.

Geography

In the Western Indian Ocean, north of Madagascar and east of Kenya, lies an archipelago of 115 exquisite islands: the Republic of Seychelles. Spread out across a vast swathe of ocean between 4°–10° south of the equator, spectacular, mist-covered peaks rise precipitously out of the glittering topaz Indian Ocean. With a dramatic landscape, a vibrant culture and a rich flora and fauna both above and below the water, the islands of Seychelles offer visitors an experience of a lifetime. Although the landmass of Seychelles is only 455 sq km (176 sq miles), the oceanic Exclusive Economic Zone (EEZ) is far greater at 1.374 million sq km (530,500 sq miles). As a biodiversity hotspot, Seychelles offers varied and incredible diving, and snorkelling experiences with fringing coral reefs that teem with life.

The Seychelles islands are divided into two main groups; the inner and outer islands. The inner islands house the majority of the population of Seychelles and are the most easily reached by visitors. There are around 41 islands in this group all of which are formed from granite with the exception of Bird and Denis, which are low-lying coral islands.

Once part of the southern supercontinent Gondwana, the granitic islands of Seychelles were formed when this landmass disintegrated some 65 million years ago. The Seychelles plateau remained in its current position creating a 'microcontinent'. This plateau stayed above sea level for a long period of isolation, allowing many endemic animals and plants to evolve.

The inner islands are the only oceanic granitic island group in the world. The largest and most visited of the islands are Mahé, Praslin, Silhouette and La Digue.

Grande Barbe on Silhouette, one of the inner granitic islands.

Anse Source d'Argent on La Digue is famous for its impressive granite formations.

Mahé

The principal and largest island of Seychelles has an area of 155 sq km (60 sq miles). It is home to the capital city, Victoria, and to the only international airport in the country. The majority of the population (90 per cent) resides on Mahé, which has perhaps the most interesting topography of the inner islands.

Praslin

The second largest island at 38 sq km (15 sq miles) lies 49 km (30½ miles) north-east of Mahé. Famed for its Coco de Mer forest, Praslin is home to one of Seychelles' two UNESCO World Heritage Sites, the Vallée de Mai. In addition, the long, curving beaches of Grande Anse and Côte d'Or offer excellent bases for diving and snorkelling.

Silhouette

Casting a striking shadow on the horizon, this is the third largest island in Seychelles at 20 sq km (7½ sq miles) but has only a small resident population and limited accommodation options. As a national park, over 92 per cent of the island is a protected area.

La Digue

Certainly one of the most charming of the inner islands, La Digue is only 10 sq km (4 sq miles) in area and offers a more laid-back experience. With only a few cars, many bicycles and even the odd ox and cart, La Digue offers a quieter destination with only 2,000 residents.

This book focuses mainly on the accessible inner islands, but if budget and time allows, some of the coralline outer islands such as Desroches, Aldabra and Alphonse also offer excellent opportunities for diving and snorkelling.

History

Known as the 'melting pot' of cultures, Seychelles is a relatively young country with a rich and interesting history. The first recorded discovery of the islands was in 1501 by João de Nova, a Portuguese explorer. But it was not until over two hundred years later, in 1770, that a group of French settlers arrived on the islands with Indian and African slaves. These early colonists established a spice industry, growing nutmeg, cinnamon and cloves. Seychelles grew over the next 40 years under French rule with Chevalier Jean Baptiste Queau de Quinssy at the helm, although there was much British interest in the islands. With the upheavals caused by the French revolution, Britain once again attempted to claim possession of the islands and in 1814 Seychelles finally came under British rule as a colony of the British Empire. The plantations of cotton and sugar cane on the islands continued to grow and by 1816, Seychelles had a population of 7,500 of whom 6,600 were slaves.

The export of copra was once a major industry for Seychelles.

With the abolition of slavery in 1835, there was an influx of freed slaves from ships captured by the British. They provided an able work force for the expanding coconut plantations on the islands, and the export of copra (dried coconut kernels from which oil is obtained) increased. Although a British colony, the islands remained heavily influenced by the French, both in language and culture. Until the Second World War the islands were dominated by the French-speaking plantation owners and Creole-speaking workers.

Later in the 20th century Seychelles experienced some dramatic changes. Many political detainees were exiled to the islands, including African Kings, Arab freedom fighters and an Egyptian Premier. The market for coconut oil and vanilla declined and the natural resources of Seychelles were heavily exploited in their place. After the Second World War ended, the political landscape of Seychelles changed with the election of the first legislative council in 1948.

In 1964 two political parties were formed, the Seychelles People's United Party (SPUP),

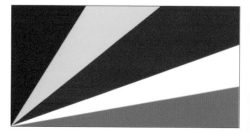

The flag of the Republic of Seychelles

embracing socialism and the independence of Seychelles, and the Seychelles Democratic Party (SDC), which was more interested in keeping close ties with Britain. In 1970, James Mancham, the leader of the SDC was elected as Chief Minister of Seychelles.

On 29 June 1976, with the support of both political parties, Seychelles became an independent nation with James Mancham as its first president. Only a year later however, whilst Mancham was out of the country, the SPUP staged an armed coup and the Seychelles became a single-party socialist state with France Albert René as president. This political situation remained in place for the next 16 years though

there were several unsuccessful coups attempting to remove René. Then in 1991, Mancham returned to Seychelles and a multi party state was recognized once again. René remained in office until 2004 when he retired and handed over to the then Vice-President, James Alix Michel. President Michel is currently still in office.

Seychelles has a growing population of around 92,000 people. Its history has led to a race of mixed ethnicities and cultures, and today's Seychellois are a cosmopolitan and proud people. Tourism and fishing (primarily of tuna) are the pillars of the economy but small-scale agriculture and local industries are also important sources of income.

Traditional fishing methods are still used in Seychelles.

Climate

Weather

Seychelles has the blissful advantage of a near-constant temperature that rarely drops below 24°C (75°F). Throughout the year, temperatures range between 24 and 32°C (75°F and 89°F). This warm, tropical climate is marked by two distinct seasons: the north-west monsoon and the south-east monsoon.

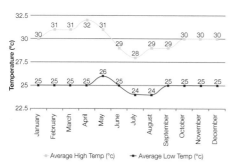

Average temperature for Seychelles by month.

The north-west monsoon runs from November to March and the south-east from June to September. Both seasons are named after the direction of the prevailing wind during these periods. The north-west monsoon brings with it heavy rains and choppy seas, interspersed with calm, sunny periods. Wind speed varies between 15 and 22 kph (9 and 14 mph) and the highest rainfall is between December and February. The south-east monsoon is cooler and drier but the wind is much stronger, with wind speeds of up to 37 kph (23 mph), leading to rough seas for most of this period.

The best weather usually comes at the changeover between these seasons, in March/April and October/November. Although not guaranteed, the weather in these months is usually fairly windless, bringing calm seas and blue skies.

Sea temperature and visibility

The sea temperature varies from 23 to 30°C (73 to 86°F) through the year with the lower temperatures during the south-east monsoon from June to September. Once the north-west monsoon arrives in October/November the temperatures start to rise, and by April the water can be a balmy 30°C (86°F). Advice on the correct exposure suit to wear for diving is given in the equipment section (see page 39).

The change in monsoon can also affect the underwater visibility. The south-east monsoon brings cold upwellings of plankton-rich water, which can reduce the visibility to only a few metres (feet). During the north-west monsoon the visibility is usually better and with the right conditions it can be over 30 m (100 ft). It is worth noting, however, that the underwater visibility is variable throughout the year and rough seas can often stir up sand and sediment particularly on the sites close to the shoreline.

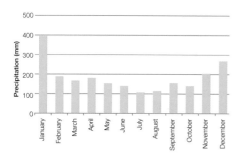

Average rainfall for Seychelles by month.

Practicalities

Language

The three official languages of Seychelles are Creole, French and English. All three languages are widely spoken throughout Seychelles, with Creole being the most commonly spoken and English usually used for written communication. Creole is a French patois. Much of its vocabulary is similar to French, although somewhat simplified, with words and phrases from other languages incorporated. It is not uncommon to hear conversations in which a mix of Creole and English words are used. English is the language of business in Seychelles and all dive centres can teach courses in English and French, as well as a range of other languages.

Getting there

By Air

Seychelles is well served by several different airlines that have varying routes to the international airport (SEZ) on Mahé Island. As of 2019 there are connections through Kenya, France, UK, UAE, South Africa and Sri Lanka.

By Sea

Cruise ships still regularly call at the port of Victoria, although this has fluctuated in recent years due to increased piracy activities in the Western Indian Ocean. The cruise ships generally visit during the north-west monsoon when the seas are calmer.

Passport/Visa

If on a short-stay holiday (a month or less), then a visitor's permit is issued by immigration on arrival in Seychelles. If necessary this permit can be extended to up to three months from the date of issue.

When arriving at immigration you will usually need to show the following documents:
- A valid return or onward ticket (if you do not have a ticket, you will be required to purchase one before being allowed to enter the country)
- Proof of accommodation in Seychelles
- Passport (valid for six months after your departure from Seychelles)

Before you depart, it is important to check with your country of nationality to see if there is any additional information or permissions needed for you to be granted a Seychelles tourist visa.

Accommodation

Seychelles offers a wide range of accommodation to suit most budgets and needs. There are the lower priced self-catering rooms and small guesthouses, slightly more expensive small to large hotels, then the higher end luxury villas and spa hotels. Some of the islands offer a 'one island, one resort' package, where there is only one hotel on the island, for that ultimate tropical island paradise experience.

On Mahé the main tourist area is in Beau Vallon, which is also the location of several dive centres. If you plan to dive every day, it is worth being based in or close to this area to save on travelling time. Other dive centres are currently located at Port Launay and Anse à la Mouche.

If you are planning to dive off Praslin Island, then the Côte d'Or area offers several dive centres and a variety of accommodation options. Grande Anse on the other side of the island has many beachfront properties and is a popular location for tourists.

La Digue is a relatively small island, therefore most locations are only a short bicycle ride away from the dive centres.

Money

The currency of Seychelles is the Seychelles Rupee (SCR) and 100 cents make up one rupee. There is a range of currency denominations in coin and note form, all of which depict beautifully the natural and cultural heritage of Seychelles.

Although foreign currency is widely accepted in hotels, guesthouses and other tourism establishments, Rupees are essential for other incidental purchases. The Seychelles Rupee is not an exchangeable currency so you can neither buy it before you arrive nor exchange it for other currencies after you leave. Therefore you will need to obtain local currency immediately on your arrival to the islands. This can be done in a number of ways: from an ATM machine using a debit card, or by exchanging foreign currency at a bank or Bureau de Change. There are facilities at the airport but they are not open 24 hours a day.

There are now ATM machines on the three main islands of Mahé, Praslin and La Digue. These machines should accept most international debit cards but note that they only pay out in local currency.

Alternatively, foreign currency cash such as US Dollars (US$), Pounds (GBP) and Euros (€) can be exchanged at the branches of the various banks operating across the three main islands. International bank branches that can be found in Seychelles are: Barclays Bank, Mauritius Commercial Bank (MCB), Bank of Baroda and Nouvobanq. There are also many Bureaux de Change that exchange foreign currency, often at a better rate than the banks. Euros are usually the preferred foreign currency, and you will often find prices quoted in this tender.

Please note: It is illegal to exchange foreign currency with anyone who is not a licensed operator. Do not exchange money with anyone who approaches you in a public place.

A number of larger establishments (hotels, restaurants, shops, dive centres) now accept payment by debit or credit card (e.g. Visa, Mastercard and sometimes American Express). However, this is not always the case and it is a good idea to check in advance of any intended purchases or bookings.

Getting around

Bus

There is a cheap public bus service operated by Seychelles Public Transport Company (SPTC), which has routes on Mahé and Praslin. Many routes service most areas of the two islands and the buses are well used by the locals. Details of the bus schedule can be obtained at the central bus station in Victoria or on the SPTC website. The buses run regularly throughout the week during the day, with a decreased service on Sundays and Public Holidays.

Taxi

Taxis are widely available throughout Mahé and Praslin, and there are now several on La Digue. There is a taxi rank in the centre of Victoria, and at the airport and the ferry port on Mahé. In addition, some of the larger hotels have a small taxi rank. Most hotels and guesthouses should be able to arrange a taxi for you, or recommend a taxi driver. Although a convenient mode of transport, taxis are relatively expensive and are most useful in the evenings when public transport is not available.

Car Hire

The roads in Seychelles can be narrow, twisting and steep but are in relatively good condition.

If you want to explore Mahé and Praslin further or will be travelling regularly, then hiring a car is a good option. It is also useful if you want to explore some of the harder-to-reach snorkel spots or have heavy dive equipment to carry.

There are many car-hire companies on Mahé but fewer on Praslin. Details of these companies can usually be obtained from your hotel or guesthouse or from a phone directory. A variety of cars is available for hire from small hatchbacks to more luxurious four-wheel drives. There are no car-hire companies on La Digue but bicycles are easily rented usually through the hotel or guesthouse and are an environmentally friendly mode of transport.

You will need to show a valid driving licence in order to hire a car and remember that in Seychelles you drive on the left side of the road!

Boat

There is a reliable ferry service from Mahé to Praslin and La Digue, and from Praslin to La Digue. Travelling in a modern catamaran, the journey takes around one hour from Mahé to Praslin, and 1 hr 15 minutes from Mahé to La Digue. There is also a smaller ferry service that operates from Praslin to La Digue. The boats are an efficient mode of transport between these inner islands and allow visitors to easily enjoy a multi-island holiday.

Plane

There are several domestic air routes, operated by Air Seychelles, between Mahé and a number of the inner and outer islands. For the purposes of this book the only route to note is Mahé to Praslin. There are several flights a day from the domestic terminal at Mahé airport to Praslin. The flight only takes around 15 minutes so is the quickest way to travel between the two islands.

Small aircraft are used for flights between islands.

The Marine Environment

The vibrant waters surrounding the 115 islands of Seychelles are home to a rich diversity of marine organisms that occupy a variety of nearshore and offshore habitats. Several of these environments are easily accessible to those visiting the inner islands of the archipelago, and offer the opportunity of close-up encounters with many of Seychelles' charismatic marine fauna.

A school of fusiliers swims over a reef of soft and hard corals.

Coastal habitats

The inner islands of Seychelles contain a number of coastal habitats. Sheltered bays harbour shallow seagrass beds, and mangrove forests are dotted across the intertidal shoreline. Beyond these lie coral reefs, often referred to as the rainforests of the sea, in recognition of the rich diversity of animals and plants that they support. Together these three interlinked ecosystems are a treasure trove of life waiting to be discovered.

Mangroves

Mangroves are found on tropical and sub-tropical coastlines between 30° north and south of the equator. They inhabit the intertidal area where, due to specialized biological adaptations, they are capable of tolerating saline conditions. Mangroves provide an important habitat for a wide diversity of organisms and play a significant role in the sequestration of carbon dioxide, storing three to five times more carbon per equivalent area than tropical forests. The shallow protected waters

Mangroves act as important nursery grounds for a wide variety of marine creatures.

around mangroves are also crucial nursery grounds for numerous marine species including commercially important fish species. People living in coastal communities around the world often rely on mangroves for food, fuel and construction materials, as well as ecosystem services, such as water filtration and coastal protection.

There are seven species of mangrove found in Seychelles, all of which are present within the inner island group. The White Mangrove (*Avicennia marina*), known as 'mangliye blan' in Creole, is perhaps one of the most common and can be seen in fringing mudflats and protected bays. Other frequently encountered species include *Bruguiera gymnorrhiza* with its misshapen aerial roots and *Rhizophora mucronata*, which has long tangled prop roots and distinctive white flowers. Though there has traditionally been little direct use for mangroves within Seychelles, many mangrove areas have been drained and cleared for coastal development. The largest remaining pockets are found at Port Launay, Anse Intendance and Anse à la Mouche on Mahé, as well as a few locations on Praslin, La Digue and Curieuse.

Seagrass beds

Seagrasses are a unique group of marine flowering plants found in shallow tropical and temperate waters. Like mangroves they provide critical ecosystem services including reducing wave action, improving water clarity and nutrient cycling. They are important feeding areas for green turtles and nursery grounds for a variety of fish and shellfish species. As they are plants and require sunlight to photosynthesize, seagrass beds prefer shallow waters.

Seagrass beds help to trap sediment and improve water quality. They are also feeding grounds for Green Turtles.

In total there are eight different species of seagrass within Seychelles. Seagrass beds are often found within the reef flat of a carbonate coral reef, otherwise known as a back reef. There are extensive seagrass beds around many of the inner islands, situated from a depth of one to around 20 m (3 to 65 ft).

Huge coral-encrusted granite boulders are found beneath the waves.

Coral reefs

Coral reefs are composed of the limestone skeletons of reef-building corals, algae and other marine organisms, deposited layer upon layer to form complex structures. They are usually found within shallow tropical waters, in areas where there is ample sunlight, warm saline water and a hard substrate to which corals can attach. Corals prefer clear seawater, so coral reefs tend to be less developed in areas with high sediment or freshwater input.

There are three types of coral reef; fringing, barrier and atoll. Fringing reefs grow seawards directly from the shore and tend to be the youngest type of reef. Barrier reefs also border shorelines but they are separated from land by an expanse of water known as a lagoon. Atolls are formed when

The Baie Ternay Marine National Park has a rich and diverse carbonate reef.

a fringing reef grows upwards around a volcano or seamount, eventually forming a lagoon as the volcano sinks leaving a ring-shaped coral atoll.

Within Seychelles' inner islands, coral reefs are fringing and can be separated further into granitic reefs and carbonate reefs, terms that will be used frequently later in this book. Seychelles is perhaps more famous for its granitic reefs, where huge granite boulders scatter the coastline and offshore granite pinnacles rise from the seabed to break the surface. These sites drop steeply to a depth of 5 – 20 m (15 – 65 ft) before giving way to sand, rubble or carbonate reef substrate. With their numerous caves, gulleys and overhangs, the coral-encrusted granite boulders provide the ideal habitat for sharks, rays and a wide diversity of reef fish. Granitic sites tend to be situated in more exposed areas where they experience strong currents and wave action resulting in a lower diversity of coral species. Dominant coral genera include encrusting Faviids and fast-growing Acroporas.

Carbonate reefs are made of calcium carbonate and in Seychelles are more commonly found within protected bays or offshore as patch reefs.

The carbonate reef is divided into various zones as shown in the diagram below. The reef flat is subjected to tidal fluctuations with some coral colonies exposed during the lowest tides. In this area high variations in salinity, temperature and light intensity act to inhibit coral growth. Despite these limiting factors certain coral species thrive here, protected from the majority of wave action by the reef crest.

The reef crest bisects the reef flat and the fore reef, and is an area of high wave intensity. It contains a ridge where a limited number of small corals, zoanthids and macro-algae are capable of withstanding the wave action.

Beyond the reef crest, the fore reef is furthest away from shore and usually slopes downwards at a steep angle. This area is home to the largest coral colonies on the reef, where they are protected from the majority of the wave action. In areas of deeper water delicate branching species grow alongside massive boulder colonies. Due to their light dependence, coral species richness is highest from 5 – 20 m (15 – 65 ft) deep, below which it begins to decrease.

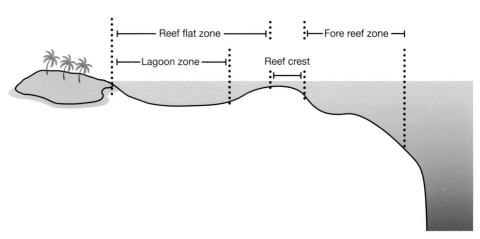

The morphology of a carbonate coral reef.

Life on the coral reef

Coral reefs are said to contain 25 per cent of all marine life on the planet, despite covering less than one per cent of the world's oceans. The coral reefs of Seychelles support over 300 species of coral and 400 species of fish.

Coral reefs are able to survive in nutrient-poor oceanic waters due to highly efficient, nutrient cycling mechanisms. The reef ecosystem revolves around the presence of symbiotic algae, known as zooxanthellae, which live within their animal host, coral. Zooxanthellae, along with phytoplankton, seaweed and seagrass, are primary producers in a complex marine food web. They are the first trophic level of the web, which supports all other life on the reef. These marine plants provide food for primary consumers or herbivores, which in turn sustain omnivores and carnivores at the top of the chain. This is a simplified description however, as in reality the picture is far more complex, with numerous stages and consumers separating the reefs' inhabitants.

Within the coral reef food web there are many different types of consumers. Detritivores, such as sea cucumbers, are at the bottom of the web and consume organic matter that has accumulated on the reef, playing a critical role in maintaining a

healthy reef ecosystem. Next are the herbivores (e.g. parrotfish, surgeonfish, turtles) that feed on algae and seagrass. Fish species can be divided into planktivores, fish that feed primarily on phytoplankton within the water column; omnivores, such as butterflyfish and triggerfish which target a variety of invertebrate species as well as algae and coral; corallivores, whose diet is made up entirely of coral; and invertivores, who prefer to pick off a variety of invertebrates from the substrate. Above all of these are the piscivores, who are fish that eat other fish and form the next level of the web. They range from the small, such as lizardfish, to the large, such as reef sharks.

The hunter and the hunted

To support such a diversity of organisms in a relatively small area, coral reef inhabitants have evolved to fill every conceivable ecological niche and developed ingenious ways to exploit their environment.

Many fish species adopt a strategy of 'safety in numbers', forming large schools that make it difficult for predators to pick out individuals. Disruptive colour patterns make this strategy particularly effective and it is common in fish that school above the reef in the water column.

Camouflage is a strategy employed by both reef fish and marine invertebrates. Predatory scorpionfish and stonefish are capable of changing colour to match their background. The effect is enhanced by the presence of numerous flaps of skin that help to break up their outline. These ambush predators wait for prey to pass by, relying on their camouflage to conceal them until the last moment when it is time to strike.

Another form of camouflage is to resemble an object of little interest. This is a strategy adopted by the juvenile forms of several fish species

The Zanzibar Butterflyfish is a corallivore, feeding only on coral polyps.

The Robust Ghost Pipefish is a master of camouflage.

including the Circular Batfish (*Platax orbicularis*), which is common in Seychelles waters. Juveniles of this species have a brown mottled colouration and are found in extremely shallow water where they often lie on their sides, resembling a floating leaf. The same approach is adopted by the Robust Ghost Pipefish (*Solenostomus cyanopterus*), which is also found in Seychelles waters. The pipefish is able to change its colour to blend in with a variety of backgrounds and often resembles a blade of seagrass or a leaf.

Mimicry can be a useful tactic for survival on the coral reef. When an edible animal resembles a noxious one avoided by predators, it is known as 'Batesian mimicry'. Usually the toxic species is more common than the mimic, which increases the chances of predator avoidance. The Black-saddled Toby (*Canthigaster valentini*) is a small poisonous reef fish. As it is distasteful, it has no reason to fear predation and remains out in the open. The juvenile of the Saddleback Grouper (*Plectropomus laevis)* closely resembles the toby, and through this mimicry is able to avoid predation without the need to hide. A secondary benefit of this strategy is that by resembling the toby, the Saddleback Grouper is able to approach its prey more easily. Mimicry is also found in marine invertebrates, juveniles of the Flowerfish Sea Cucumber (*Pearsonothuria graeffei)*, for example, resemble a toxic, sponge-eating nudibranch to help deter predators.

Reef relationships

With many different species living in close proximity on coral reefs, it is no wonder that some have evolved close physical relationships. These relationships are known as symbiosis and occur in three different ways: mutualism, commensalism and parasitism.

Mutualism is a relationship between two organisms in which both benefit from the presence of the other. The very existence of coral reefs is built upon a mutually dependent relationship between coral and photosynthetic algae known as zooxanthellae. The zooxanthellae live within the tissue of the coral polyps, where they receive protection from predation along with

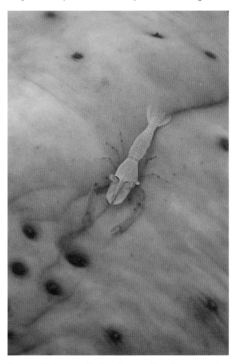

Emperor Shrimps can be found on a variety of sea cucumber species, with whom they have a commensal relationship.

compounds necessary for photosynthesis. In return the zooxanthellae provide the coral with glucose and amino acids, which the coral then uses to make carbohydrates, fats and proteins used to build a calcium carbonate skeleton.

Commensalism is where two species interact to the benefit of one of the species but without any negative effect to the other. Several species of sea cucumber found in Seychelles waters have a commensal relationship with the Emperor Shrimp (*Zenopontonia rex*). These small shrimp are transported by the sea cucumber and therefore exposed to new food sources without the need to expend energy. While the sea cucumber does not receive anything in return, it is not adversely affected by the presence of the shrimp.

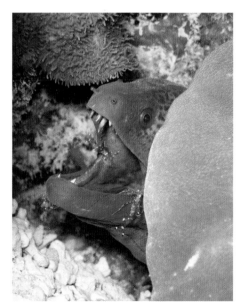

A Giant Moray is attended to by cleaner shrimps.

Parasitism is less common than mutualism or commensalism. Parasitism occurs when one species benefits from the relationship to the detriment of another. On coral reefs, isopods provide a good example of parasitism. These marine crustaceans attach themselves to reef fish and while some do not cause their hosts any harm, others can prevent the uptake of nutrients and cause the fish discomfort.

Cleaning stations

Many fish utilize the services of 'cleaning stations' on the reef to have dead skin and parasitic organisms removed. Cleaning stations are found throughout the reef and are essential to the maintenance of a healthy ecosystem. A number of marine organisms, including both fish and invertebrates, provide services at these stations. In return for removing unwanted parasites, the cleaners receive a meal as well as immunity from predation. The Bluestreak Cleaner Wrasse (*Labroides dimidatus*) is a common sight at cleaning stations where it can be found removing parasites from the gill filaments of reef fish. There are also several species of cleaner shrimp found on Seychelles reefs, which remove parasites and dead skin from moray eels, groupers and other fish species.

Day and night

The majority of reef fish are diurnal, meaning they are active during daylight hours. During the day sunlight penetrates through the ocean's upper layers, allowing reef fish to use their vision

A parrotfish encased in a mucous bubble.

as a means of seeking food and avoiding prey. Many reef fish have excellent vision and their brightly coloured bodies are a testament to the importance of sight in species recognition and visual cues.

For many of the fish active during the day, night is a dangerous time, with predatory species on the lookout for a meal. Diurnal species, heavily reliant on sight, are placed at a significant disadvantage during the darkness of night. Many predators hunt by smell and the best defence strategy for most reef fish is to hide within the coral recesses. Some species, such as the Chevroned Butterflyfish (*Chaetodon trifascialis*), adopt a nocturnal colouration in an attempt to blend in with their background. Other fish, like the parrotfish, lodge themselves under corals and encase themselves in a mucous bubble. The mucus is produced from special glands behind the gills and it is thought that the protective cocoon keeps out blood-sucking parasites.

At night plankton rise from the ocean depths providing a feeding bonanza for numerous fish and invertebrate planktivores that remain hidden during the day. Assemblages of squirrelfish and soldierfish feast on the plankton in the water column, while feather stars, shrimp and other invertebrates sieve plankton from the current as it drifts by. Coral polyps also capitalize on the vertical migration of the plankton by emerging from their limestone structures to feed. Invertebrates tend to be nocturnal, spending the day hiding underneath rocks and coral heads before appearing at night to feed. The Spanish Dancer (*Hexabranchus sanguineus*) is a large nudibranch that is predominantly nocturnal, preferring to emerge at night to feed on sponges. The species is common in Seychelles and is often encountered on night dives.

Many predatory fish are more active at night, preferring to rest during the day when they are easily outmanoeuvred by reef fish that are able to see them approach. Whitetip Reef Sharks (*Triaenodon obesus*) are by far the most common shark species encountered by divers within the granitic inner island group. During the day they are often found lying in caves or beneath ledges, but by night the sharks cruise the reef searching for fish amongst the corals.

What's in a name?
The Spanish Dancer has the extraordinary ability to swim to avoid predation. The rhythmic undulation of the nudibranch's vibrant red-and-white mantle closely resembles that of an exotic Spanish dancer, giving rise to the animal's common name.

On night dives Spanish Dancers can sometimes be seen 'dancing'.

Marine conservation and research

Seychelles has a long history of marine conservation and was at the forefront in the drive to identify coastal areas to set aside for protection. This was an important act of foresight

Prolonged elevated sea temperatures can cause coral bleaching, turning coral colonies white as zooxanthellae are expelled.

Outbreaks of Crown-of-thorns Starfish can lead to extensive damage of coral reefs.

as coral reefs and marine life globally have faced an increasing number of threats over the past 50 years.

Threats to coral reefs

In 1998 abnormally high sea temperatures, caused by the El Niño/Southern Oscillation interacting with the Indian Ocean Dipole, triggered a mass coral bleaching event causing high levels of coral mortality in many places with significant damage to the reefs of Seychelles. Within the inner islands some reefs suffered a decline in coral cover of up to 90 per cent; areas that were previously covered by complex reef structures were reduced to rubble.

Coral bleaching occurs when the sea surface temperature increases and zooxanthellae are expelled from coral tissue, which leads to a breakdown in the symbiotic relationship between them. As a result the coral loses its pigment and appears bright white or 'bleached'. Although they may look dead, bleached corals are still living and if elevated temperatures subside within a short time, zooxanthellae will return to the corals and they will survive. Unfortunately, as was seen in 1998, if sea surface temperatures remain high for a prolonged period of time, the zooxanthellae do not return to the coral and the colony dies.

Bleaching is not the only threat. In December 2004 an earthquake occurred in the Aceh region of Indonesia. The tsunami that followed was one of the most powerful seen in over 40 years and affected several countries across the Indian Ocean, resulting in over 168,000 casualties in Indonesia alone. In Seychelles the force of the tsunami had dissipated significantly before it arrived and fortunately the human casualties were low. This was in part due to the coastal protection offered by coral reefs and mangroves within the islands. Post-tsunami monitoring surveys indicated Seychelles coral reefs had suffered substantial structural damage, particularly to the northern and eastern islands, where up to 50 per cent of reefs were affected.

In recent years, the Crown-of-thorns Starfish (*Acanthaster planci*) has caused localized damage to coral reefs around Mahé and Praslin Island. Crown-of-thorns Starfish are voracious coral predators but they are also a natural part of the coral reef ecosystem in low densities. The starfish is, however, subject to population explosions and during such a time can kill vast areas of coral. The triggers for these population booms are unknown, but may be linked to the removal of their natural predators or the increased loading of nutrients into coastal waters. Dedicated removal programmes by local stakeholders are undertaken when there are signs of an outbreak, in an effort to mitigate the effects of this predator.

In the years that have passed since the 1998 bleaching event and the 2004 tsunami, the reefs of the Seychelles inner islands have again undergone a remarkable transformation. In some areas the recovery of the reefs has been impressive. Sadly this outstanding recovery has not been uniform and not all reefs have improved at the same impressive rate. Nature's capacity to recover is extraordinary, but the growing list of human threats makes it increasingly difficult for coral reefs to bounce back.

Land reclamation and coastal development continue to stress reef environments, while the demand for reef fish from the local population and the burgeoning tourist industry are contributing to a decline in near-shore fisheries. On a global scale, ocean acidification and warming seas pose real long-term threats to coral reef recovery and the probability and severity of further mass bleaching events are likely to increase.

With tourism as one of the two pillars of the Seychelles economy, the health of the islands' coral reefs is critical. Today a number of local and international organizations are actively involved in marine research and conservation initiatives within Seychelles.

Marine National Parks

The Sainte Anne Marine National Park (MNP), listed in 1973, was the first designated marine park in the Western Indian Ocean. The Sainte Anne MNP comprises six islands located 5 km (3 miles) east of Victoria and covers a total area of 1,385 ha (3,422 acres). Since the creation of this MNP several more have been designated, including Port Launay and Baie Ternay MNPs on Mahé Island, Curieuse MNP, Ile Cocos

MNP and Silhouette Island MNP. In total the Marine National Parks of Seychelles cover an area of approximately 3,500 ha (8,650 acres). Responsibility for managing the MNPs lies with the parastatal organization, Seychelles National Parks Authority (SNPA).

Certain regulations and conditions are legislated for Marine National Parks in order to protect these important areas. Tourists entering a MNP will be required to pay a fee to SNPA, which is usually built into the cost of any excursion by tour operators, and these fees go towards the maintenance and patrolling of the parks. Boats are requested to use the mooring buoys provided or to anchor in designated areas so as not to damage the coral reefs within the MNPs. All motorized water sports are banned from MNPs, including water skiing and the use of jet skis. Finally, it is stipulated that all those using the park should respect all marine life. This means that all types of fishing are prohibited, as is the collection of shells, plants or any other marine life.

In addition to the MNPs, a number of islands are categorized as 'Special Reserves', which gives protection to the waters that surround them. These islands are managed by national and international NGOs.

Aride Island, a Special Reserve.

Cousin Island Special Reserve is managed by Nature Seychelles, a national NGO. The island is home to internationally significant seabird breeding populations as well as endemic land birds. The beaches of Cousin Island remain an important nesting site for the critically endangered Hawksbill Turtle (*Eretmochelys imbricata*).

Located 16 km (10 miles) north of Praslin, Aride Island is the most northerly of the granitic islands. Like Cousin it is of international importance for breeding populations of seabirds. The beaches and coral reefs surrounding the island are protected as a Special Reserve, and the island is currently under the management of the Island Conservation Society.

D'Arros Island is situated 255 km (159 miles) south-west of Mahé, and is part of the Amirantes Island group. In 2012 D'Arros was purchased by the founder of the Save Our Seas Foundation (SOSF) and has applied for Special Reserve status. The foundation is now undertaking research projects both on the island and its adjacent atoll, St Joseph.

Aldabra Atoll is located over 1,000 km (621 miles) to the south-west of Mahé and is a Special Reserve that was declared a UNESCO World Heritage Site in 1982. Seychelles Islands Foundation (SIF), a public trust, has managed the atoll since 1979. Due to its remote location and decades of protection, Aldabra offers an insight into an ecosystem that has been relatively untouched by humans. It has several unique endemic terrestrial species, including the world's largest population of Aldabra Giant Tortoises (*Aldabrachelys gigantea*) as well as a healthy marine ecosystem that is dominated by large predators. The atoll also has the largest nesting population of Green Turtles (*Chelonia mydas*) in Seychelles.

Coral reef monitoring

Global Vision International (GVI) is an international community development and conservation organization, which is registered as an NGO in Seychelles. It works closely with the SNPA to monitor the coral reefs of north-west Mahé. Since 2004, international volunteers have joined the GVI programme to be trained in species identification and coral reef monitoring techniques. The data collected by GVI is shared with SNPA, then used to assess the long-term health of the reefs.

A number of other organizations are undertaking small-scale coral reef monitoring programmes on Mahé and other islands. Nature Seychelles' 'Reef Rescuers' programme began in 2010 and aims to restore coral reefs around Cousin Island through 'coral gardening' and replanting of coral fragments back onto the degraded reef. The project aims to transplant 50,000 fragments of coral, which have been grown in underwater nurseries around the island.

Whale sharks

Each year during the south-east monsoon, cold upwellings bring nutrient-rich waters to the coastline of the islands on the Mahé plateau. In September and October Whale Sharks (*Rhincodon typus*) usually arrive to feed on this plankton bonanza. Whale sharks are the largest

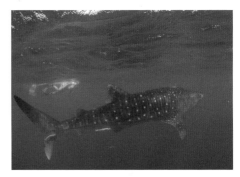

The harmless Whale Shark is the biggest fish in the sea.

fish in the ocean, reaching a length of over 12 m (39 ft). They feed on zooplankton, sieving huge quantities of jellyfishes and crustacean larvae from the water. Found throughout tropical and temperate seas, these gentle giants tend to congregate off the west coast of Mahé before disappearing along with the plankton at the arrival of the north-west monsoon in November.

The Marine Conservation Society Seychelles (MCSS) has been monitoring Whale Sharks and recording data on their activities and movements in Seychelles since 1996. Although protected in Seychelles waters since 2003, fisheries in other parts of the world target these highly migratory species for their fins, and the IUCN Red List of Threatened Species lists the Whale Shark as 'Vulnerable'.

Marine turtles

There are five species of marine turtle that have been recorded in Seychelles, but it is only the Hawksbill Turtle and the Green Turtle that come ashore to nest on the archipelago's beaches. Green Turtles are more common within the outer islands and in particular on Aldabra Atoll, whilst Hawksbill Turtles are more regularly encountered within the inner granitic islands. The Green Turtle is listed on the IUCN Red List as 'Endangered', while the Hawksbill is listed as 'Critically

Endangered'. The Hawksbill Turtle population in Seychelles is the largest remaining within the Western Indian Ocean (Mortimer, 1984), and is one of only five populations worldwide that still have more than one thousand females nesting annually (Meylan and Donnelly, 1999).

Seychelles did have a long tradition of harvesting turtles. Up until the mid 1990s, Green Turtles were caught for their meat and their 'calipee', the glutinous layer of fat found beneath the shell, which is considered to be a delicacy. Hawksbill Turtles were less favoured as a food source due to the presence of biotoxins within their flesh. Instead they were harvested for their shells, which were used to make ornaments and jewellery.

In 1994 the Seychelles government passed a law making it illegal to kill, possess or eat turtle meat. Although small-scale poaching does still occur, the main threats to turtles in Seychelles have now shifted to coastal development, pollution and entanglement in fishing equipment.

Whilst poaching and coastal development have reduced the number of Hawksbill Turtles visiting the beaches of Mahé and Praslin, there are still several beaches on both islands where they can be seen nesting. A number of islands have important Hawksbill nesting populations, including

Hawksbill Turtles still nest on many of the beaches of the inner islands.

The younger generation take an active role in events such as the Seychelles Sea Turtle Festival.

Bird, Cousin, Cousine, Curieuse and Silhouette. In fact Cousin's protection as a Special Reserve has led to an eight-fold increase in the number of nesting turtles in the past 40 years. Some of these islands are privately owned, while NGOs or government departments manage others, and all have some form of turtle monitoring programme. In 2013 a group of individuals working on turtle conservation within Seychelles, organized the first Seychelles Sea Turtle Festival to raise awareness of marine turtle conservation issues. This brought together many of the organizations working in turtle conservation within Seychelles for the first time. The festival is now an annual event (usually in the second week of August) and has the support of both the Seychelles Ministry of Environment and Energy, and the Ministry of Education.

Seychelles has taken conservation and protection of its natural environment seriously for many years, both through government action and the activities of NGOs. This foresight has paid dividends and the marine environment has shown resilience in the face of some serious and continuing impacts. The future of Seychelles relies on a balancing act between the necessity for sustainable development and the growth of the tourism sector, alongside the need to protect the coastal environment, which holds such a wealth of biodiversity.

Seychelles Ocean Festival
(formerly known as SUBIOS)
In 1989 the SUBIOS (Sub Indian Ocean Seychelles) Underwater Film and Image Festival was set up to promote Seychelles' underwater world and to better inform the local population about the incredible diversity of marine life in Seychelles' waters. Over the years the festival has grown into a major event and today attracts visitors from all around the world. The event was renamed as the Seychelles Ocean Festival in 2015, and usually takes place in the final quarter of the year when it provides an opportunity to learn more about the Seychelles marine environment.

Green turtles can be encountered on Seychelles reefs.

Diving and Snorkelling in Seychelles

Seychelles offers some incredible diving and snorkelling opportunities, but to ensure that you get the most from these experiences a little preparation is required. This chapter covers some of the most important aspects you should consider, to make sure that your underwater adventure is safe and enjoyable.

Sainte Anne Marine National Park.

Health and safety

Pre-travel

Medical fitness

It is recommended that you have a full medical examination before undertaking any scuba diving activity. Although you may feel physically fit and healthy, there might be an underlying medical condition that could affect your ability to scuba dive. Despite being a fun and relaxing activity for many, scuba diving does put your body under physical pressure and stress, so it is important to get checked out first to put your mind at ease. All dive centres should ask you to complete a medical questionnaire before diving and this will give you the opportunity to discuss any concerns you may have regarding your fitness and ability to dive.

While it is not necessary to have a medical examination prior to snorkelling, it is advisable to make sure that you have a good level of fitness and that you are an able swimmer before embarking on any snorkelling activities. Snorkelling can be a strenuous activity even in calm waters, and sea conditions can change quickly.

Vaccinations and malaria

There are relatively few diseases that visitors to Seychelles need to be vaccinated against. It is recommended that travellers have vaccinations for hepatitis A, hepatitis B, tetanus and typhoid. A yellow fever certificate is required for all travellers over one year of age arriving from an infected area.

Malaria is not normally known to occur in Seychelles, so malaria prevention medication is not needed. However, precautions against insect bites should be taken as there have been occasional outbreaks of dengue fever, which is transmitted to humans through mosquito bites.

Advice should always be sought from a health-care professional before your visit.

Insurance

Snorkelling is not usually considered a hazardous activity and should be covered under any standard travel insurance policy. If you are unsure of the details of your policy, it is best to check with your insurance provider before you travel.

If you are planning to go diving, it is crucial that you have an insurance policy with appropriate cover. Many travel insurance policies do not automatically cover scuba diving, so make sure you check with your insurance provider before taking out a policy. DAN (Divers Alert Network) offers travel insurance policies that are designed with divers in mind and they can be easily purchased online.

It is recommended that you have adequate insurance cover for any emergency medical treatment that might arise when in Seychelles, including emergency evacuation. Make sure that you bring the relevant documentation with you.

Medical treatment

If you feel unwell, have a cold, or just feel very tired, then it is best not to push yourself and you should take a day off from diving or snorkelling. It is your own responsibility to look after your physical health, and diving or snorkelling when you are not 100 per cent fit poses a risk to both your health and safety.

Should you need to seek medical treatment, then the main hospital in Seychelles is in Victoria, Mahé. This hospital has an Accident and Emergency centre and can provide emergency medical care for serious health issues. There are also smaller hospitals on Praslin and La Digue.

For minor health problems there are several doctors' clinics across Mahé, Praslin and La Digue, which will provide basic medical care to tourists and appointments can usually be made at short notice. It is a good idea to bring a basic first aid kit with you (e.g. painkillers, seasickness tablets, mosquito repellant). There are also well-stocked pharmacies on Mahé and Praslin where non-prescription medications can be purchased.

Hazardous marine life

The marine environment of Seychelles is home to an abundance of marine creatures, including a small number of species that should be treated with caution. Whether snorkelling or diving you should avoid touching, standing on or coming into close contact with any of the marine life you encounter. Although serious hazardous marine life injuries are rare, should you come into contact with any of the following marine animals, the described first aid care below will assist in reducing any discomfort:

Urchins These spiny echinoderms are found on both coral reefs and seagrass beds. They can be well camouflaged and most species have sharp spines that can become embedded in the skin. If injury does occur, immerse the area in hot water for at least 30 minutes, as this will dissolve the spines. If possible remove the remaining spines taking care not to break any. Pain and swelling can sometimes occur and antibiotics may be needed if an infection is suspected.

One of the most cryptic echinoderms is the

Flower Urchin (*Toxopneustes pileolus*), a species that covers itself in coral rubble making it difficult to spot. Hidden behind its delicate, flower-shaped spines is a potentially dangerous toxin. If contact is made, follow the same procedure of immersing in hot water.

A local remedy for sea urchin wounds is to rub papaya on the affected area. An enzyme within the papaya juice will help to break down the urchin spines.

Razor clams Hidden in the sandy substrate of seagrass beds, these bivalves have a razor sharp edge to their shell, which if stepped on can cause a deep cut. Always wear reef shoes or dive booties when walking on seagrass beds. If injured by a razor clam, exit the water immediately and seek medical attention if necessary.

Jellyfish In Seychelles these ocean drifters are more prevalent in the south-east monsoon, though they can be encountered all year round. The Portuguese Man-o-war (*Physalia physalis*) has a gas-filled air sac, which floats on the water's surface, and long trailing tentacles. It is a distinctive purple colour and the tentacles can give a painful sting. During rough sea conditions the species often washes up on shore. If stung, remove any tentacles and flush the area with vinegar for at least 30 seconds. Once the reaction

The toxic Flower Urchin is often covered in debris.

Portuguese Man-o-war can be washed onto beaches during rough weather.

has subsided, apply hydrocortisone cream daily until any discomfort has been alleviated. In the event of a serious allergic reaction to the sting seek medical attention as soon as possible.

Fire coral Tan brown in colour, this coral is covered in fine white hairs that cause a burning sensation if touched. Maintaining good buoyancy and avoiding contact with the reef should keep you out of harm's way. If you do accidentally touch the coral, then flush the area with vinegar for at least 30 seconds.

Coral If by accident you do come into contact with coral then make sure to clean the wound thoroughly as soon as possible. Keep disinfecting the wound regularly and check for infection. It is advisable to stay out of the water until the wound has healed, in order to speed up the recovery process.

Scorpionfish/Stonefish This includes several species of fish, all of which are poisonous and capable of giving a sting. These 'chameleons of the sea' are usually so well camouflaged it is hard to spot them. The poison is administered from a gland at the base of the dorsal fin spines and can be extremely painful. If stung, immerse the area in very hot water for at least 30 minutes as this will break down the protein-based venom. If any spines are present, remove carefully taking care

not to break off any in the skin. Pain and swelling is common and antibiotics may be needed if an infection is suspected.

Stingrays Stingrays can often be found resting on sand or in seagrass. If walking in shallow water, make sure to shuffle your feet so as to disturb any rays, and always look where you are walking. In the event that you are stung by a ray, remove the barb (if there is one) and immerse the affected area in hot water for 30 minutes.

Sharks Incidents involving sharks and people in Seychelles are extremely rare. Sharks are unlikely to act in an aggressive manner unless threatened. Never corner or try to handle a shark, as even the smallest reef shark is capable of causing a painful bite if molested.

Sea conditions

Seasickness

All of the diving in Seychelles is undertaken by boat. On calm, windless days this can mean many happy hours spent on deck, enjoying the thrill of being on the ocean. However, calm conditions are never guaranteed and at certain times of the year you may encounter rougher seas, which can bring on seasickness. This condition can come on quickly and unexpectedly, even to those who are not usually susceptible to it. Factors such as the smell of engine fumes, too much sun, or tiredness can all lead to the onset of seasickness.

There are many types of seasickness medication available but these should be used with caution. Some medications can cause drowsiness as a side effect, and this can be dangerous when diving. You should always ensure that you use a non-drowsy seasickness medication if planning to dive. Many divers use natural alternatives such as sweets or ginger to help alleviate the symptoms of nausea. You should also stay out of the sun, drink

Well camouflaged scorpionfish can be hard to spot.

Most dive sites and snorkel spots are accessed by boat.

plenty of water and look at the horizon. Quite often once underwater, the nausea will subside.

If severe seasickness sets in you should consider cancelling any subsequent dives until the symptoms have passed, and you are sufficiently rehydrated.

Likewise with snorkelling, many trips are at locations that are only accessible by boat. It is less of a risk to take seasickness medications that cause drowsiness but it is still preferable to seek a non-drowsy alternative. As you can often be on the boat for several hours, if you are prone to seasickness and notice that the sea is choppy you may wish to reschedule your trip.

Sunburn

At only 4° south of the equator, the tropical sun in Seychelles is extremely strong and it is highly recommended that you act 'sun safe' at all times. Take sunscreen with you on the boat if diving, ready for the surface interval, and if snorkelling remember to wear a T-shirt or rash vest (a type of tight, lycra, quick-dry T-shirt) and apply sunscreen everywhere else. Time can slip by when you are entranced by the marine life and sunburn can develop all too easily. Drink plenty of water before and after your activity, you will be surprised at how quickly the sun can dehydrate you.

Currents and tides

The warm tropical waters around Seychelles appear inviting but care should always be taken when entering the water. Strong currents can be found at several dive and snorkel sites and care should be taken in relation to the tides and the sea conditions. When diving, your guide should advise you of any strong currents or surges you may encounter during the dive. Make sure you stay close to your buddy and your dive guide, if you should get separated follow the lost buddy procedures given in your dive briefing. Always carry a Delayed Surface Marker Buoy (DSMB) and inflate it on your ascent, to alert the dive boat to your position.

Low tide in Baie Ternay Marine National Park.

When snorkelling with a guide, they will advise of any adverse conditions and as with diving, stay close to your guide and follow their instructions. If snorkelling on your own, pay close attention to the strength and direction of any currents or tides before and during your snorkel. Check online or with your guesthouse for a tide timetable so you can plan your snorkel around the incoming tides. In certain areas there are often strong currents. It is a good idea to ask your hotel or guesthouse for advice before embarking on your snorkel trip.

Boats

With many locals and visitors alike enjoying the azure coastal waters of Seychelles, there are sometimes many boats passing through diving and snorkelling areas.

When diving, make sure that you stay with your guide and surface with them if possible. If you are separated for any reason then deploy a Delayed Surface Marker Buoy (DSMB) on your ascent to alert any boats to your presence.

Greater caution needs to be applied when snorkelling. If snorkelling from a boat stay close to the boat or your snorkel guide where possible, and try not to become separated from the group. Should you decide to go snorkelling on your own from shore, stay as close as possible to the shoreline and remain vigilant of passing boats and jet skis. Remember that a snorkeller on the surface can be hard to spot from a boat, particularly at certain times of the day.

Hyperbaric chamber (Diving only)

Provided that you dive within your limits and follow the advice of your dive centre professionals, the risk of developing Decompression Sickness (DCS) is minimal. When scuba diving, every diver has a responsibility to follow the direction of their dive guides and not take unnecessary risks. It is advisable not to dive under the effects of alcohol, drugs, dehydration, ill health or certain prescription medications. If you have any doubts about your fitness to dive you should consult with a medical professional before diving.

If you feel unwell or have any signs or symptoms of DCS after diving (see inset box) then medical attention should be sought immediately. You may wish to contact your dive centre initially to discuss your condition and ask their advice. If DCS is suspected, then you should be placed on oxygen immediately and if symptoms persist, transferred to the hyperbaric chamber at Victoria hospital on Mahé or Silhouette Island for further treatment. Each dive centre should always have an oxygen kit on board their boats and at the dive centre. Transfer to the hyperbaric chamber on Silhouette Island is usually made by boat or helicopter.

To make the most of your snorkelling experience remember to follow some basic safety precautions.

Decompression Sickness (DCS)

Decompression Sickness (DCS) is also known as 'the bends' and is the result of inadequate decompression following exposure to increased pressure, for example, an uncontrolled ascent at the end of a dive. In some cases, the condition is mild and not an immediate threat. In other cases, serious injury does occur; and then the quicker treatment begins, the better the chance for a full recovery.

During a dive, the tissues in the body absorb nitrogen from the air you are breathing, in proportion to the surrounding pressure. As long as you remain at pressure, this does not present a problem. If the pressure is reduced too quickly, however, the nitrogen comes out of solution and forms bubbles in the tissues and bloodstream. This occurs more commonly when the dive table or dive computer limits have been breached, but it can also occur even when all guidelines and advice have been followed.

Bubbles forming in or near joints are the presumed cause of the joint pain experienced in a classic case of DCS. When high levels of bubbles form, complex reactions can take place in the body, usually in the spinal cord or brain. Numbness, paralysis and disorders of higher cerebral function may result. If large numbers of bubbles enter the venous bloodstream, congestive symptoms in the lungs and circulatory shock can then occur.

Symptoms of DCS
• Unusual fatigue
• Skin itch
• Pain in joints and/or muscles of the arms, legs or torso
• Dizziness, vertigo, ringing in the ears
• Numbness, tingling and paralysis
• Shortness of breath

Signs of DCS
• Skin may show a blotchy rash
• Paralysis, muscle weakness
• Difficulty urinating
• Confusion, personality changes, bizarre behavior
• Amnesia, tremors
• Staggering
• Coughing up bloody, frothy sputum
• Collapse or unconsciousness

Note: Symptoms and signs usually appear within 15 minutes to 12 hours after surfacing; but in severe cases, symptoms may appear before surfacing or immediately afterwards. Delayed occurrence of symptoms is rare, but can occur, especially if air travel follows diving. (Taken from www.diversalertnetwork.org 'Decompression Illness: What is it and What is The Treatment?')

5 things to remember when diving
• Get checked out by a doctor before diving
• Make sure to take out sufficient insurance cover
• Maintain neutral buoyancy on your dives and do not touch any marine life
• Always dive within the limits of your experience and training
• Drink lots of water, sleep well and stay out of the sun

5 things to remember when snorkelling
• Always tell someone where you are going, never snorkel alone
• Wear a life jacket if unconfident
• Make sure you leave the water before sunset
• Do not overestimate your ability
• Check your position regularly, and swim back to shore if you find yourself drifting too quickly

Equipment

Having the right, well-fitting equipment can make all the difference to your snorkelling and diving experience. It is worthwhile taking some time to ensure that you get the best equipment for your needs so that you are comfortable and happy in the water.

Be sure to check your equipment before you descend underwater.

One of the first questions is whether you want to purchase your own equipment or whether you want to hire some when you arrive in Seychelles. The dive centres should be able to provide you with most of the equipment that you need for diving or snorkelling, while the larger hotels should have snorkelling equipment for hire. If you are planning on undertaking a significant amount of diving or snorkelling during your visit, and if you want to make sure that you have equipment that fits really well, you should consider purchasing some basic items before your trip. In the event

that you want to buy equipment in Seychelles, then some items can be purchased from certain shops in Victoria, or from dive centres on Mahé and Praslin. Be aware that the selection is limited and items may be more expensive than elsewhere.

Diving

Divers with their own equipment should make sure to get it serviced before their trip. Some of the dive centres are able to carry out basic repairs, but for a hassle-free holiday, it's worth taking the time to get equipment thoroughly serviced beforehand.

If you are a relatively new or first-time diver, it is best just to buy the basic equipment (mask, snorkel, fins, wetsuit) or hire it at a dive centre in Seychelles, which can be a better option if you are not sure that you want to make the investment in lots of equipment. Bear in mind though, that this equipment may not fit you perfectly, so you may be more comfortable in your own. Advice on some of the essential items of equipment is given below.

Mask and snorkel

Although you can hire a mask at the dive centre, if you are thinking of snorkelling or diving often, it is worth investing in your own good quality mask. Make sure you try the mask on before buying to check it fits well.

Your mask is your window to the underwater world, therefore it is of great importance to make sure that it doesn't become fogged underwater. To prevent condensation forming on the inside of your mask, a good tip for new masks is to rub toothpaste or baby shampoo on the inside of the lenses. Repeat this for the first few times that you use the mask, remembering to rinse it out just before your dive or snorkel. This should stop condensation forming inside the mask, and provide you with a nice clear view. After that spit usually works fine but some masks need a reapplication of toothpaste or shampoo every so often. If you have a moustache then make sure to trim it closely and apply some Vaseline. This will form a seal between the moustache and mask, and prevent water from entering the mask.

Unless you are planning on doing lots of snorkelling as well, then a basic snorkel is sufficient for diving purposes. This can be hired with a mask at the dive centre.

Fins
Most dive centres offer full foot fins for hire. These do not require the additional use of dive booties and are easily taken on and off. In the warm waters of the tropics these fins are excellent for diving and snorkelling. Ensure that you use a pair that fit comfortably and are not too tight or loose. If you wish to buy your own fins, you may

Ensuring your equipment is comfortable and safe is the first step for any underwater experience.

consider half-foot fins, which require dive booties but are suitable for both temperate and tropical conditions. Dive booties are also useful for some of the snorkel sites where you have to walk across seagrass beds.

Wetsuits
With the sea temperature varying throughout the year, the type of wetsuit necessary to remain comfortable will also change. The table below gives recommendations on the thickness of wetsuit to use throughout the year, however this may vary between individuals.

Month	Wetsuit recommended	Average Underwater temperature (° C)
January	3mm shortie	28
February	3mm shortie	28
March	3mm shortie or no wetsuit	29
April	3mm shortie or no wetsuit	30
May	3mm shortie or no wetsuit	29
June	3mm long	26
July	3 or 5mm long	25
August	3 or 5mm long	24
September	3mm long	26
October	3mm long	26
November	3mm long	27
December	3mm long	27

Tanks and weights
All dive centres provide dive cylinders and weights so you will not need to bring your own. Most dive centres use 11 litre aluminium cylinders with yoke valves. If you have a regulator with a DIN valve, the valve can usually be changed by the dive centre, although it may be worth bringing an adaptor with you to make this transition easier.

Different sized tanks are sometimes available with prior booking. Some dive centres also offer Nitrox air fills.

Other useful items
- A **dry bag** for carrying valuable items to the boat from shore
- **Toothpaste** or **baby shampoo** for keeping your mask de-fogged
- A **tank banger** to alert your dive buddy to anything amazing that you see underwater
- A **Delayed Surface Marker Buoy** (DSMB) and reel are good to have in the event of an emergency
- A **dive computer** is not essential but is useful for accurately monitoring your own dive plan
- An **underwater camera** (see section below) is a great way to capture your underwater experience and to help you later identify the many animals you will see.

Snorkelling

Your equipment needs for snorkelling are much simpler than for diving. Just grab a mask and snorkel, a pair of fins, and a T-shirt or rash vest, and you are ready to go! Snorkelling gear can be easily hired from any of the dive centres or some of the larger hotels. However, you may want to invest in a few of these items yourself so you have more freedom as to where and when you can snorkel. Whether you hire or buy, give yourself some time to get used to the equipment before you dive into the ocean. For first time users this equipment can feel quite cumbersome and alien, so try it out in shallow water before venturing out further.

For advice on mask, snorkel and fins please see information in the diving section above. It is worth adding that you should try to hire or buy a snorkel that has a splash guard at the top and a purge valve at the bottom. This will help prevent water from entering your snorkel, and allow you to blow water out more easily.

Other useful items
- **Toothpaste** or **baby shampoo** to keep your mask de-fogged.

- **Wetsuit booties or reef shoes** can protect your feet at snorkel sites where you will need to walk out across seagrass beds to the reef at low tide. Bear in mind that these shoes will not usually fit in full foot fins, so you will need to carry them during your snorkel.
- A **waterproof watch** is useful for keeping track of the time. Once you are immersed in the underwater world time can fly, and you don't want to miss the bus back to your hotel!
- An **underwater camera** (see section below) is a great way to capture your underwater experience and help you identify the many marine creatures you will encounter.

Underwater photography

Being able to capture your underwater experience is now very easy with a wide range of underwater cameras on the market. These products are not readily available in Seychelles so it is recommended that you purchase them before your visit.

Seychelles reefs offer plenty of attractions for the underwater photographer.

Below is a short overview of some of the more commonly used types of camera systems, but it is worth doing your own research.

Underwater cameras fall into three main categories – housing systems, amphibious/waterproof cameras and video cameras.

Housing systems consist of a plastic or metal case that a normal digital camera can be placed inside. The housing creates a waterproof and pressure-resistant case for your camera. These housings are usually effective to 40 m (130 ft) and therefore are the most appropriate option for scuba-diving activities. Housings are not available for every model of digital camera so you will need to check compatibility. Alternatively you can purchase a camera and housing as a package.

Amphibious or waterproof cameras are digital cameras that do not have any exterior casing, which makes them small and light. Different models are waterproof to different depths, with some models waterproof to 25 m (80 ft). These cameras are ideal for snorkelling or on the boat but are not always suitable for diving as some models are only usable to relatively shallow depths.

Video cameras are also becoming a more popular choice amongst divers and snorkellers. Brands such as GoPro offer small cameras that can take both videos and photographs. These are sold with underwater cases and are easily placed into a BCD pocket or attached to a retractable pole for ease when snorkelling. There are many different types of accessories that you can add on to these cameras including a red filter, fish-eye lens and LCD screen.

Once you have become more familiar and experienced with using a camera underwater, you may wish to upgrade your equipment or purchase additional strobe lights.

Colourful soft corals are an excellent subject for underwater photographers.

Top 5 tips for underwater photography
• **Get close to your subject.** This minimizes the amount of water you are photographing through which improves the colour and contrast of your photographs. Approach your subject slowly and be aware of your surroundings.
• **Be patient.** Remember to take your time and think about how best to frame your shot. Sometimes taking a few extra minutes can reward you with a much better quality of photograph.
• **Shoot upwards.** If you shoot upwards towards the sea's surface your photograph will usually have a better perspective. If you aim down then your subject will often have a flat appearance and blend into the background.
• **Use the camera's underwater mode.** As you descend underwater light is lost, in particular the red wavelength of light. The underwater mode on your camera adds more red to your photographs so they will not all appear green/blue. Once you descend to below a few metres you should also use the flash. This provides more light and therefore will yield more accurate colours in your photograph.
• **Show some scale.** Sometimes it is hard to tell from a photograph how large an object is underwater, it is a good idea to add a subject that will show some scale.

Certification and experience

The PADI diving certification is offered at dive centres in Seychelles.

Diving

There are many diving certification agencies available worldwide. In Seychelles the following certification agencies are currently available; Professional Association of Diving Instructors (PADI) and Confédération Mondiale des Activités Subaquatiques (CMAS).

PADI is probably the most widely recognized agency worldwide and it is usually possible to find a PADI dive centre in most diving destinations. They offer a straightforward certification system that can take you from beginner to professional instructor. CMAS is most widely used in Europe and is the oldest certification agency. They have a different level system from most other agencies based on attaining a number of stars.

If you will be taking a dive course for the first time, or you wish to further your certification level, take some time to discuss your certification options with your chosen dive centre, and make sure you are comfortable with the dive instructor who will be leading your course. Divers certified with another certification agency will still be able to dive in Seychelles. Just make sure that you bring your certification card with you as proof of your level of ability.

Snorkelling

Although there are no official snorkelling certification organizations or courses, it is important that you evaluate your own level of experience and skills first, to ensure you have the best snorkelling experience. A guide to levels of snorkelling experience is given below:

Beginner You have never snorkelled before but are a reasonable swimmer. If this is you, make sure that an experienced snorkeller or guide accompanies you at all times. Practise snorkelling in shallow water until you have gained more confidence. Do not be frightened to use a flotation device until you are a bit more experienced.

Intermediate You have snorkelled before and are comfortable with the snorkelling equipment. You should still make sure that you are accompanied by another experienced snorkeller but you could try some of the deeper snorkel spots or snorkelling boat trips.

Advanced You are able to float on the sea's surface, are confident snorkelling and can duck dive to shallow depths. Again you should never snorkel on your own but you are certainly ready to enjoy any of the snorkelling spots that Seychelles has to offer, dependent on sea conditions.

Whatever your level, it is essential that you stay within your comfort level at all times and never snorkel alone.

Types of diving facilities

There are several options available for diving in Seychelles. These include shore-based independent dive centres, dive centres attached to hotels, liveaboards and yacht charters.

Small powerboats are used by independent dive centres to reach the dive sites.

Large yachts can be chartered for day trips or longer periods.

Independent dive centres

If you are happier staying on land, or just want to do a couple of dives, then the independent dive centres are the best option. They mainly offer diving around Mahé, Praslin and La Digue. All diving is done from small powerboats and the dive sites are usually divided into 'short distance' and 'long distance'. The dive centre can confirm the classification of each particular site but needless to say, the long-distance sites incur an additional charge for the extra fuel required to reach them. Most of these centres operate a daily schedule of a double dive in the morning and a single dive in the afternoon, every day of the week. Night dives are usually available on request. This may vary though, and specific times and days should be confirmed with the dive centre. Multiple dive packages are usually available and the dive centre staff often speak several languages. If taking a dive course then you may be able to request the course materials in a language of your choice. Some of the dive centres also have Nitrox available as long as you book ahead.

Hotel dive centres

A few of the hotels have dive centres attached to them, which operate under the same principles as above.

Liveaboards

What better way to experience the beauty of Seychelles, than to sail around the islands diving en route. There are several liveaboard boats that operate in Seychelles and they offer an all-inclusive experience where all food, accommodation and diving are catered for on board. The tours vary in length and there are several different routes taken. Some of the itineraries are based solely around the inner islands with diving off Mahé, Praslin, La Digue and other islands in between. During the north-west monsoon certain boats offer trips to some of the outer islands, such as the Amirantes and Aldabra groups.

Yacht charters

If you would rather have some privacy on your holiday but still want the freedom to explore the islands by boat, then you can charter a yacht for your diving trip. Although more expensive than other diving options, you will have the freedom to choose when and where you dive and the route you take. Again the routes taken are influenced by the sea conditions, but you should be able to provisionally negotiate them in advance. The charter companies will usually provide the equipment, but cylinder fills will need to be done at dive centres along the way.

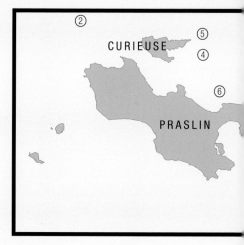

② ⑤
④

CURIEUSE

⑥

PRASLIN

⑱ NORTH ISLAND

⑯

SILHOUETTE ISLAND

⑰

Indian Ocean

⑫

⑪

⑥ ⑨

Glacis

Anse Etoile

⑭ ③ ⑧ Beau Vallon

① ⑮
Bel Ombre

Bel Air ● ● Victoria
Mont Fleuri ●

⑩ ⑤
④

Port Launay

⑦

Port Glaud

Les Mamelles ●

Cascade ●

Grand Anse

MAHÉ

Pointe la Rue ●

⑬

Anse Aux Pins ●

Anse Boileau ●

Au Cap ●

② Anse à
la Mouche ●
● Anse

● Baie Lazare

Takamaka ●

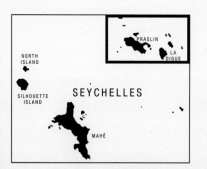

NORTH ISLAND

PRASLIN

LA DIGUE

SILHOUETTE ISLAND

SEYCHELLES

MAHÉ

Guide to Dive Sites

Diving in Seychelles is an unforgettable experience with turquoise waters, enthralling marine life and dazzling coral reefs. This chapter should give you a taste of the fantastic dive sites that the inner islands have to offer. This is by no means an exhaustive list, but presents a selection of some of the most popular and frequently visited sites. There are many more magnificent sites to visit that are not included here.

Key to highlights at each site

 Shark

 Turtle

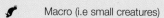 Macro (i.e small creatures)

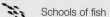 Schools of fish

 Ray

 Coral

 Soft coral

 Wreck

KEY TO DIVE SITES

Mahé
1. Aldabaran
2. Alice in Wonderland
3. Aquarium
4. Cap Matoopa
5. Baie Ternay Marine National Park
6. Brissare Rocks
7. Conception Island
8. Coral Garden
9. Dragon's Teeth
10. Grouper Point
11. L'ilot
12. Shark Bank
13. Stork Patch
14. Twin Barges
15. Whale Rock

Silhouette & North Island
16. Anse Mondon
17. Grande Barbe
18. Sprat City

Praslin & surrounding islands
1. Ave Maria
2. Booby Rock
3. Channel Rock
4. Coral Garden
5. Point Rouge
6. St Pierre
7. South Marianne Island

Maps showing location of dive sites.

Mahé

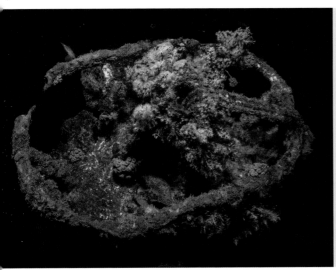

Aldabaran

- Reef type: Wreck
- Level: Advanced
- Depth: 35–40 m
  (115–130 ft)
- Snorkelling: no
- Rating: ★★★

The colourful, coral-encrusted wreck of the *Aldabaran*.

There are a small number of wrecks that can be dived in Seychelles and the *Aldabaran* is certainly one of the finest. The *Aldabaran* was an old fishing vessel that was intercepted by the Seychelles coastguard whilst illegally fishing in Seychelles waters. The coast guard confiscated the boat, and in 2008 the 28-m (92-ft) vessel was deliberately sunk to provide a new dive site close to Beau Vallon bay. The vessel now sits intact and upright in 40 m (130 ft) of water, with her upper deck at approximately 25 m (82 ft) below the surface. The wreck lies close to the coastline on a sandy bottom in an otherwise empty landscape. The area is subject to strong currents and the descent to the wreck is usually taken down the dive boat's anchor line.

Over the years the ship has been colonized by a variety of marine life, and today colourful sponges and soft corals encrust the entire surface of the vessel. Take your time to look closely as hidden amongst this dense cover are small shrimps, nudibranchs and gobies. The wreck acts as a beacon to pelagic fish, such as jacks, which are a common sight as they swim past looking for prey. Resident schools of yellow snapper swirl like confetti around the ship's upper deck, at times obscuring the scene with a curtain of gold. Lionfish hunt juvenile reef fish amongst the rigging, while expertly camouflaged scorpionfish lie motionless on the deck, waiting to ambush their prey.

Due to its depth, this is certainly a site for the more advanced diver. You will have a short bottom time and it is important to keep an eye on your dive computer so as not to exceed your safe dive limits. A single circuit of the ship should take around ten minutes, at which point your dive computer will be signalling for you to begin your ascent. As you make your way to the surface remember to keep your eyes open for any passing barracuda and Wahoo.

Alice in Wonderland

- Reef type: Carbonate
- Level: Beginner
- Depth: 4–18 m (13–60 ft)
- Snorkelling: yes
- Rating: ★★★★
- 🐢 🐟 🪸

Fields of *Acropora* coral at Alice in Wonderland.

Alice in Wonderland is situated on the west coast of Mahé Island in Anse à la Mouche bay. A carbonate reef only five minutes by boat from the beach, the dive site starts at a depth of 4 m (13 ft) and drops down to 18 m (59 ft).

This extensive coral reef is one of the finest around Mahé Island with an excellent diversity of corals. Fields of *Acropora* spp. lie next to huge *Porites* spp. colonies and luxuriant leather corals. In amongst the coral, plentiful brightly coloured reef fish make their homes. Angelfish and butterflyfish are particularly abundant, as are surgeonfish and bristletooths.

Juvenile Whitetip Reef Sharks are often found hiding underneath the coral bommies. These small sharks prefer the protection offered by the coral on carbonate reefs and tend to migrate to the granitic sites as they grow larger and need more space.

'Alice' is also an excellent site for turtle encounters, and both Green and Hawksbill Turtles can be seen here. As with all the dive sites within the inner islands, Hawksbill Turtles are more common and they are often found resting on the reef or feeding on sponges lodged beneath the coral. Green Turtles are found in fewer numbers around Mahé and tend to be more wary of divers, but can sometimes be approached closely when they are sleeping on the reef. Other inhabitants include octopus, which glide across the reef in search of a meal, changing colour as they go and blending in effortlessly with their background.

Depending on the time of year, visibility at this site varies from 5 – 25 m (15 – 80 ft). The relatively shallow depth and absence of strong currents, means that Alice in Wonderland is a site suitable for divers of all abilities.

Aquarium

- Reef type: Carbonate
- Level: Beginner
- Depth: 5–12 m (15–40 ft)
- Snorkelling: yes
- Rating: ★★★

Soldierfish school above the reef at Aquarium.

Aquarium is a popular dive site on the north coast of Mahé Island, a short distance from most of the dive centres in Beau Vallon. The site consists of two large carbonate coral heads covered in a variety of hard corals, and as its name suggests it has an abundance of small, brightly coloured, reef fish.

The coral embankments start at a depth of 12 m (40 ft) and rise to within a few metres of the surface. They harbour a wealth of marine life that it usually takes most of the dive to explore. If you have some time to spare, there is a patchy carbonate reef surrounding the coral heads. This area also deserves some investigation and you might be rewarded with a sighting of an Indian Ocean Walkman. The shallow depth and lack of currents makes Aquarium an excellent site for beginner divers and it is often used as a training site by local dive centres.

For those with a little more experience, there is still plenty of marine life on offer. Large schools of soldierfish hover in the water column as gaudily coloured angelfish dart in between fissures in the reef. Moray eels are also common, their heads poking out between the corals, mouths opening and closing as they push water over their gills. Slender pipefish move gracefully over the reef hiding in the maze of corals. Octopus are often seen here as well, so keep your eyes peeled as these well-camouflaged animals can be hard to spot. After an enjoyable dive the safety stop is usually spent hovering above one of the coral mounds, where you can watch the dazzling array of reef fish below.

Seychelles Anemonefish are often seen at Aquarium.

Cap Matoopa

- Reef type: Granitic
- Level: Intermediate
- Depth: 12–20 m
  (40 – 65 ft)
- Snorkelling: no
- Rating: ★★★★
-

Characteristic granite boulders at Cap Matoopa.

Situated on the north-west coast of Mahé Island, Cap Matoopa overlooks the Conception channel between Mahé and Conception Island. It is a granitic site with large boulders piled beneath the surface, forming a labyrinth of caves and overhangs. The maximum depth of the site is 20 m (65 ft), below which the sandy bottom continues sloping towards the middle of the Conception channel, which reaches depths of 50 m (165 ft). The dive usually starts with the granite boulders on your righthand shoulder, and progresses towards the mouth of the channel. This granitic site, like many on the north-west coast of Mahé, is relatively exposed and can only be dived at certain times of the year when the sea is calm enough.

Owing to the many hiding places created by the granite boulders, Cap Matoopa is an excellent site to see Whitetip Reef Sharks. Although they are sometimes observed swimming above the reef, more frequently they can be found resting underneath the boulders in small groups. It is possible to approach them closely but take care not to disturb them, as any sudden movement will cause them to swim off. It is not just the Whitetips that spend time during the day resting under the granite rocks, Nurse Sharks are also regular visitors, as are Marble Rays, which can grow up to 1.8 m (6 ft) in diameter.

There is a good diversity of fish life at this site with plenty of surgeonfish and snapper leisurely swimming around the rocks. High in the water column schools of batfish and chub feed off plankton, while Bumphead Parrotfish occasionally pass through. Due to the strong wave action at this site the coral cover here is patchy, with some areas harbouring large branching coral colonies while in others the corals are confined to a thin layer encrusting the boulders.

Depending on the strength of the current, the dive normally finishes at the point of the channel where the shoreline turns to the north. The three-minute safety stop takes place in the blue, away from the reef, and is perfect for watching eagle rays as they fly past you.

Baie Ternay Marine National Park

- Reef type: Carbonate
- Level: Beginner
- Depth: 4–18 m (13–60 ft)
- Snorkelling: yes
- Rating: ★★★★★

A panoramic view of Baie Ternay Marine National Park

The exquisite Baie Ternay Marine National Park is located on the north-west coast of Mahé Island. Declared a national park in 1979, it can only be accessed by boat. From Beau Vallon, it's a 15-minute boat ride. The coastline bordering the marine park is covered by dense vegetation interspersed with granite boulders and small deserted beaches. Oceanic currents rarely affect this protected bay and this, coupled with the shallow waters and diverse marine life, makes it an ideal site for divers of all abilities.

Shallow, lush seagrass beds give way to a magnificent carbonate coral reef, rich in both hard and soft corals. The coral cover here is excellent and the biodiversity is one of the highest within the inner islands. A variety of butterflyfish and angelfish dart among the coral heads where a good number of groupers can be found guarding their territories. These inquisitive, predatory fish can often be observed at cleaning stations soliciting the services of resident cleaner wrasse.

Baie Ternay is one of the best sites on Mahé to see marine turtles, with both Hawksbill and

Green Turtles frequently observed resting on the coral or swimming above the reef. More often than not, the turtles are oblivious to divers who make a slow approach, and will happily continue to go about their business. Juvenile Whitetip Reef Sharks also make this site their home, and are regularly encountered resting under coral outcrops, while adults are sometimes seen swimming out in the open.

The Baie Ternay Marine National Park can be split into three separate dive sites, one located at each side of the bay and a third in the centre. On either side of the bay coral-covered granite boulders give way to a carbonate reef. The site in the middle of the marine park contains the healthiest coral; the dive starts at around 5 m (15 ft) and follows the reef down to around 16 m (52 ft) in depth. For those wishing to go deeper, there is a second smaller reef found at 25 m (80 ft) but the majority of marine life is located at shallower depths.

Also found within the bay is the stunning white sand beach of Anse du Riz, which is popular for day trips that incorporate diving and snorkelling with a beach barbecue. The reef in front of the beach starts at a shallow depth, before sloping down to around 14 m (46 ft). Divers can expect to see healthy coral and plenty of small reef fish in this area.

Baie Ternay has a diverse and vibrant coral reef.

Brissare Rocks

- Reef type: Granitic
- Level: Intermediate
- Depth: > 20 m (65 ft)
- Snorkelling: no
- Rating: ★★★★★
-

Schooling snappers are a common sight at Brissare Rocks.

Located close to its sister site, Dragon's Teeth (see page 56), Brissare Rocks is one of the premier dive sites within the inner islands. Granite boulders rise above the water's surface to form a rocky outcrop, below which is an impressive reef with an amazing diversity of marine life.

Similar to Dragon's Teeth, Brissare Rocks has an abundance of both hard and soft corals that blanket the granite boulders to a depth of around 20 m (65 ft). At Brissare everything seems to be present in far greater numbers than at any other site, with schools of fish encountered at every turn. Tightly packed schools of yellow snapper are found in vast numbers alongside a wide variety of other reef fish. Expansive branching corals provide shelter to thousands of rainbow-coloured damselfish and anthias, while beneath every granite boulder cleaner wrasse groom Spotted and Oriental Sweetlips.

Whitetip Reef Sharks are particularly common at Brissare and it is not unusual to see multiple individuals on a single dive. Other large reef inhabitants include Humphead Wrasse, Bumphead Parrotfish and Hawksbill Turtles. One of the highlights of any dive here is to watch the numerous jacks hunting glassfish on the reef. They hunt as a pack, taking it in turns to break off and dart torpedo-like into the schools of glassfish, causing them to scatter in all directions.

If conditions are good and the sea is calm, it is possible to swim through the granite boulders from one side of the reef to the other. At a depth of 5 m (16 ft) the boulders are stacked in such a way that they have formed a large swim-through. The shallow depth allows for shards of light to penetrate into the channel illuminating the batfish that gather inside.

With visibility often exceeding 30 m (100 ft), Brissare Rocks is without doubt a world-class dive site. The reef and fish life are spectacular, and there is always the chance of encountering pelagic animals, such as large schools of barracuda, tuna or dolphins. Located a short distance offshore, it is only accessible at certain times of year when the sea is calm. Dive centres in Beau Vallon usually visit Brissare Rocks between October/November and April/May, although trips can be taken at other times if conditions allow. With a depth of around 20 m (65 ft) and occasional strong currents, this a site recommended for intermediate divers and above.

The swim-through at Brissare is accessible when the sea is calm.

Conception Island

- Reef type: Granitic
- Level: Intermediate
- Depth: > 18 m (60 ft)
- Snorkelling: no
- Rating: ★★★★

A diver takes in the splendid reef at Conception Island.

Up until the 1970s, Conception Island located north-west of Mahé was a coconut plantation, but today it is uninhabited and has one of the few populations of the Seychelles White-eye, an endemic and increasingly rare bird. Despite an area of 0.6 sq km (¼ sq mile), this granitic island does not have any beaches and its steep granite slopes rise precipitously from below the water's surface. This dramatic topography and undisturbed coastline, however, offers some fantastic diving opportunities.

Perhaps the most popular of these is Conception Arena. On the north point of the island, the granitic reef forms a natural underwater arena with striking boulder formations and swim-throughs. It has excellent coral cover and there is no lack of fish life, with the reef dropping down to a depth of around 18 m (60 ft) where it turns into sand. Conception South is another popular site and is of a similar structure to Conception Arena.

Like many of the granitic sites, Whitetip Reef Sharks are regularly encountered here, either swimming above the reef or resting under

the boulders. During the right season Whale Sharks can sometimes be sighted here, or in the Conception channel as you cross over from Mahé. Squadrons of Eagle Rays are frequent visitors and it is not unusual to see over a dozen individuals swimming in formation. As well as a diversity of reef fish, Conception is one of the best sites to see both Humphead Wrasse and Bumphead Parrotfish. Large herds of the latter are extremely rare now, but groups of five or six individuals are often encountered breaking off fist-sized chunks of coral from the reef as they feed.

Currents can sometimes be strong around Conception and the direction of the dive will often depend on how the current is running. The powerful currents and surge make these sites more suitable for intermediate divers. Due to its location this island is not usually dived during the south-east monsoon.

Over the last few years the coral reef at Conception has recovered significantly from the bleaching event that damaged many of Seychelles' reefs in 1998.

Coral Garden

- Reef type: Carbonate
- Level: Beginner
- Depth: 9 – 15 m
  (30 – 50 ft)
- Snorkelling: yes
- Rating: ★★★

Coral Garden has a diverse range of hard and soft corals.

Located in Beau Vallon bay only a short boat ride from the local dive centres, Coral Garden is a carbonate reef suitable for divers of all abilities. The reef is located at a depth of 15 m (50 ft) and is a mixture of hard coral and leather corals interspersed with sandy patches. Depending on the time of year, visibility can range from 5 – 25 m (15 – 80 ft) and there is usually little current.

The coral cover at Coral Garden is impressive with a good diversity of large, healthy colonies. A mixture of branching and massive corals creates a complex reef structure that shelters a wealth of marine life. This pretty reef has plenty of small reef fish, including butterflyfish and angelfish, and the occasional medium-sized grouper. Neon-coloured parrotfish and wrasse dart among the corals as flashes of pink, green, blue and yellow. In addition to the ubiquitous reef fish, Coral Garden is a great place to see Hawksbill Turtles. They can often be found resting under table corals, or with their head in the reef searching out a meal. Unlike their Green cousins, Hawksbill Turtles do not seem to mind the presence of divers and will often allow you to approach closely.

Other potential highlights at Coral Garden include the prospect of finding juvenile Whitetip Reef Sharks hiding under coral bommies or torpedo-shaped squid hanging above the reef. Coral Garden is a relaxing dive that offers the opportunity to take your time and enjoy the scenery without having to worry about strong currents or reaching your dive limits. This is a good site for beginners and also those who wish to improve their underwater photography skills in a relaxed environment.

Hawksbill Turtles are commonly found feeding on the reef at Coral Garden.

Dragon's Teeth

- Reef type: Granitic
- Level: Intermediate
- Depth: > 23 m (75 ft)
- Snorkelling: no
- Rating: ★★★★★

Delicate sea fans are found at Dragon's Teeth.

Dragon's Teeth is a granitic site that rises from around 23 m (75 ft) to just above the surface of the water. Located a few kilometres to the north of Mahé Island alongside its sister site Brissare Rocks (see page 52), Dragon's Teeth is a 30-minute boat journey from the dive centres in Beau Vallon. The site is only dived when conditions are calm, which is usually in October/November and April/May. On account of its exposed offshore location and occasional strong currents, visibility is good and regularly exceeds 30 m (100 ft). This site is suitable for intermediate and advanced divers because of its depth and the chance of strong currents.

Descending underwater down the dive boat's anchor line, you will see granite boulders smothered in both hard and soft corals. Delicate white gorgonian fans, which are rare around Mahé, grow to an impressive size and jut out from the boulders into the water column. Many species of reef fish are found at Dragon's Teeth, but like Brissare they seem to be in much greater number than elsewhere around Mahé. Clouds of damselfish surround every head of coral, while schools of fusiliers crowd above the reef in a never-ending procession. In amongst the chaos, hundreds of yellow snapper in tightly packed schools drift above the reef.

It is not just smaller marine life that is found here. Good sized groupers are common at Dragon's Teeth, as are Whitetip Reef Sharks, which are often seen swimming lazily through the schools of yellow snapper. Painted Lobsters jostle for space under the granite boulders, while lionfish hang motionless above. Make sure to look out into the blue during your dive and you may be rewarded with a sighting of large schools of barracuda or even some dolphins.

Depending on the current, a 50-minute dive is generally long enough to make a circle of the site. Starting at depth, the normal dive route is to corkscrew towards the centre of the reef ending in the shallows where the safety stop is often spent watching the Spotted Eagle Rays glide below the surface.

On a clear day when the current is running, Dragon's Teeth can put on a spectacular display, the impressive abundance of reef fish and frequent sightings of pelagics make it one of the premier dive sites within the inner islands.

Large schools of barracuda can be seen at offshore sites such as Dragon's Teeth.

Grouper Point

- Reef type: Granitic
- Level: Intermediate
- Depth: > 30 m (100 ft)
- Snorkelling: yes
- Rating: ★★★★

The dramatic landscape at Grouper Point offers some exciting dives.

Grouper Point, or 'Lighthouse' as it is sometimes called, is a granitic site situated on the western point of the Baie Ternay Marine National Park. Located at the tip of Cap Matoopa, the site is exposed and can be subject to occasional strong currents and surge. Grouper Point offers a dive experience that is unpredictable and enthralling.

The reef starts directly below the surface and drops down to a depth of approximately 30 m (100 ft). The dive usually begins inside Baie Ternay, then continues towards the Conception channel. At the point of Baie Ternay, the currents are strongest and large schools of black snapper, chub, jacks and batfish swirl in the water column. Squadrons of eagle rays are often encountered and occasionally Mobula Rays have been seen passing through. This point is usually a hive of activity, so, depending on the strength of the current, try to take this section slowly to ensure you don't miss anything.

Large granite rocks, encrusted in hard corals, provide many overhangs and small caves. Whitetip Reef Sharks are a common sight and are frequently seen swimming among the boulders, or hiding underneath, with several lying together under ledges. The granitic boulders also provide excellent cover for several species of fish. During the south-east monsoon, the visibility is reduced due to the arrival of cold, plankton-rich water. During this time Grey Reef Sharks regularly visit, and large schools of jacks are encountered.

With its abundance of pelagic species and large reef fish, it is easy to overlook the smaller inhabitants of Grouper Point. However, macro enthusiasts will not be disappointed as this site caters for everybody. The reef is home to several endemic Seychelles anemonefish, which share their host anemones with delicate Porcelain Crabs. Leaf Scorpionfish are also regularly sighted with white, yellow and brown variants all found.

Between August and October each year Whale Sharks congregate in the Conception channel and the surrounding waters. Although it is by no means guaranteed, Grouper Point offers one of the best opportunities to observe one of these gentle giants whilst diving.

L'ilot

- Reef type: Granitic
- Level: Intermediate
- Depth: > 18 m (60 ft)
- Snorkelling: yes
- Rating: ★★★★

L'ilot is famous for its beautiful soft corals.

Situated to the north of Beau Vallon bay is the small granitic islet of L'ilot. Only 100 m (330 ft) from Mahé Island, this collection of rocks with a few spindly palm trees is an essential stop on everyone's dive itinerary. A short journey by boat from local dive centres, L'ilot is a popular site that is accessible throughout the year.

The majestic boulders that emerge above the water are equally impressive below, where they are festooned with brightly coloured soft corals. Strong currents often sweep past the islet bringing with them a variety of pelagic species. The granitic boulders have formed several small caves and overhangs, where Giant Sweetlips, and sleeping Whitetip Reef and Nurse Sharks can be found.

The granitic reef is dominated by soft corals and sponges, creating a wonderful kaleidoscope of colour that is unlike any other site around Mahé. The boulders give way to a sandy bottom at around 18 m (60 ft), though much of the marine life is found at shallower depths. Schools of resident yellow snapper, soldierfish and bigeye are plentiful, while Bumphead Parrotfish sometimes visit the reef to feed.

It is not just the megafauna brought in on the current that makes L'ilot so appealing; it is also famous for its abundant macro life. Pinkeye Gobies hover above branching *Acropora* spp. corals, pausing occasionally to rest on the tips. Brightly coloured anemones shelter anemonefish and symbiotic shrimps, alongside Porcelain Crabs filter-feeding plankton from the passing current. L'ilot is also an excellent location for spotting nudibranchs with several species commonly found on sponges and soft corals. The psychedelic *Nembrotha lineolata* in particular is common here, while it appears to be scarce on other reefs in Seychelles.

Depending on the time of year, the visibility can vary widely at L'ilot as can the currents. Regardless of the direction of the current, the dive will lead you in a circle around the islet and the abundance of both larger pelagics and unusual macro subjects means that L'ilot is always a thrilling dive.

Shark Bank

- Reef type: Granitic
- Level: Advanced
- Depth: 18 – 30 m
  (60 – 100 ft)
- Snorkelling: no
- Rating: ★★★★

Snappers are found in abundance at Shark Bank.

A 20-minute boat journey from Beau Vallon bay, Shark Bank is situated 8 km (5 miles) north of Mahé, towards Silhouette Island. This exposed site is only dived during calm weather, with the best time of year to visit being in October/November and March/April.

Shark Bank is an impressive underwater granite plateau lying at a depth of almost 30 m (100 ft). Outcrops of granite rocks litter the sea floor creating a maze of gullies and passages. Whitetip Reef Sharks and sleeping Nurse Sharks are sometimes encountered here, although perhaps not as often as the name suggests. Gigantic Marbled Rays are regular visitors and are one of the highlights of Shark Bank, as are the schools of pelagic fish such as Blackfin Barracuda and Dogtooth Tuna that cruise by in the blue.

This site is perhaps most famous for its large schools of yellow snapper that blanket the reef. Numbering in the hundreds of thousands, several resident schools sweep the site parting only when a diver or shark swims though them. Coral cover at this site is limited owing to its exposed location

and strong currents. There are plenty of reef fish however, with a reasonable diversity of species found close to the granite boulders. Shark Bank is definitely more about the big stuff though, and this offshore location offers an excellent opportunity to see some megafauna up close.

Due to a constant depth of 18 – 30 m (60 – 100 ft) the dive time for this site is usually about 35 minutes, if using a dive computer. After circling the deep-water rocks divers return to the boat using an anchor line. Strong surface currents often wash over the site, therefore it is important to hold on to the anchor line so you do not become separated from the rest of the group. The strong currents combined with the depth, mean that this is a site for advanced divers only.

For the more adventurous diver, Shark Bank's remote and unprotected location offers an adrenalin rush and the opportunity for some exciting interactions with Seychelles' larger marine inhabitants.

Stork Patch

- Reef type: Granitic
- Level: Intermediate
- Depth: 5 – 25 m
  (15 – 80 ft)
- Snorkelling: no
- Rating: ★★★★

Large sea stars decorate the granite boulders at Stork Patch.

Stork Patch is a submerged granite plateau lying several kilometres offshore to the west of Mahé Island. The maximum depth is approximately 25 m (80 ft) and the reef is frequently subjected to strong currents, making it a site for advanced divers only. Just below the surface granite boulders ascend from the seabed, forming numerous canyons and underwater passages. The plateau is characterized by the branching *Acropora* spp. corals that cover the boulders and the substrate. Each coral provides refuge to plentiful damselfish that quickly disappear amongst its branches when a predator or diver approaches.

Like many of the offshore sites around Mahé Island, Stork Patch offers the chance to encounter pelagic species. Large swirling schools of barracuda are regularly observed, as are Dogtooth Tuna and the occasional Giant Trevally. Whitetip Reef Sharks cruise around the boulders while a quick inspection of the overhangs and fissures will turn up more Whitetips, Nurse Sharks and stingrays.

The main attraction at Stork Patch is without doubt the Grey Reef Sharks. Although sightings are by

no means guaranteed, Stork Patch offers one of the most reliable encounters with this species around Mahé Island. Grey Reef Sharks are an inquisitive species and will often make a couple of close passes before departing. They appear to be more common in the latter half of the year, though there have been sightings year round.

Descent to the site is usually made down the boat's anchor line and depending on the marine life a circular direction is taken around the rocks. The dive finishes on top of one of the granite boulders at around 5 m (15 ft), where thousands of sweepers envelop the corals. Schools of batfish are common as are needlefish, which can be seen hunting near the surface.

Visibility ranges from 10 – 30 m (35 – 100 ft) depending on the time of year. It is easier to reach Stork Patch from the south of Mahé, with trips taken from Dive Resort Seychelles based in Anse à la Mouche. As this is an offshore site, trips are only made when the sea is calm and the best time of the year tends to be October/November and April/May.

Twin Barges

- Reef type: Wreck/ Carbonate
- Level: Beginner/ Intermediate
- Depth: 8 – 23 m (26 – 75 ft)
- Snorkelling: yes
- Rating: ★★★★

Fish hover above the shallow wreck at Twin Barges.

Twin Barges comprises two wrecks lying close together that were deliberately sunk in 1989 to provide a new dive site. They are located adjacent to the Corsaire reef, a five-minute boat ride from Beau Vallon beach.

You will usually start the dive on the deeper of the two wrecks, descending down a mooring buoy line attached to the vessel. This barge sits upright on the sand at 16 – 23 m (52 – 75 ft) depth. Over the years the surface of the vessel has become heavily encrusted in colourful corals, soft corals and sponges, and there is little surface remaining that has not been colonized. Wire corals spiral out from the wreck and gorgonians sway gently in the current. The heads of many Geometric Moray eels can be seen inquisitively poking out of holes in the wreck. Schools of large jacks are frequent visitors to the barges where they hunt above the decks.

After 15 minutes on the deep wreck it will be time to move onto the second, shallower barge. Using the guide rope between the two vessels, the second barge is found at a depth of 12 – 15 m (40 – 50 ft) with its bow pointing towards the shore. The coral formations on this wreck are greater in abundance and the centre of the boat is more intact. Inside the barge there are many resident lionfish that hunt the thousands of glassfish, whilst trumpetfish quietly stalk their prey.

Both barges are a macro hunter's delight, with Leaf Scorpionfish regularly sighted on or near the shallow barge while frogfish, which are rare within the Seychelles inner islands, are also occasionally found. The surfaces of the barges are a particularly productive area for finding a variety of nudibranch species. Venturing out to Twin Barges at night offers the chance to discover some nocturnal reef life, such as parrotfish sleeping in their mucous bubbles and a wide variety of crustaceans.

To circumnavigate both barges, 40 minutes is usually sufficient and this leaves enough time to explore the interesting adjacent carbonate reef. Staring at a depth of 10 m (33 ft) the reef slopes upwards towards the shore and contains a fascinating mixture of hard and soft corals.

Whale Rock

- Reef type: Granitic/ Carbonate
- Level: Beginner
- Depth: > 12 m (40 ft)
- Snorkelling: yes
- Rating: ★★★
-

At Whale Rock vivid Arceye Hawkfish can be seen resting on corals.

Named after the sizeable granite rock in the centre of the dive site, Whale Rock is a splendid site for divers of all abilities. Only a short boat ride 10 minutes from the Beau Vallon dive centres, Whale Rock is a shallow site of approximately 14 m (46 ft) depth and home to a wonderful array of marine life.

Around the central granite boulder and rocky shoreline, bright orange tubastrea corals cover the rocks in a blaze of colour. Delicate gorgonians hang onto the granite surface sifting plankton from the current. Doe-eyed pufferfish swim clumsily through the water column whilst Bigeye Breams hang motionless above the rocks.

Whale Rock is a great site for underwater photography, particularly for those who like macro subjects. Cryptic Leaf Scorpionfish are common but careful searching is needed to find them. Gaily coloured Peacock Mantis Shrimp scurry across the reef to their burrows, while Painted Lobster hide under corals waving their antennae. Swimming away from the coastline, garden eels can be seen sticking out of the sand. If you

approach them slowly you might get a chance to see them up close before they disappear into the substrate. Due to the prevalence of macro subjects and its shallow depth Whale Rock is also an excellent site for night dives.

This dive site is exposed to the elements during the north-west monsoon and as a result it is best visited between March and November.

Yellow variation of the Guineafowl Puffer.

Praslin and surrounding islands

Ave Maria

- Reef type: Granitic
- Level: Intermediate
- Depth: > 20 m (65 ft)
- Snorkelling: no
- Rating: ★★★★

The impressive Ave Maria dive site.

Ave Maria is a dive site located to the east of Praslin and north of La Digue, and is visited by dive centres from both islands. This small granite islet is home to a handful of trees and palms, as well as numerous terns, which nest on the exposed granite rocks.

Below the water's surface, the granite boulders drop to a depth of around 20 m (65 ft) where they give way to a sandy seabed. The coral cover is excellent, with large colonies of *Pocillopora* spp. surrounded by hundreds of damselfish jostling for space with abundant soft corals. The rocks form a complex network of swim-throughs and overhangs where a variety of grouper species wait to ambush their prey.

A dive at Ave Maria usually entails a circular tour of the island, with the direction determined by the prevailing current. In the shallows, close to the islet, schools of surgeonfish and Blue and Yellow Fusiliers dart by high in the water column.

Descending further onto the reef large schools of Bengal Snapper form tightly packed balls, whilst goatfish rummage for prey in the sand.

Ave Maria is an excellent site for encountering pelagics, make sure to keep an eye on the blue where schools of mackerel and batfish frequently pass by. Larger residents of the reef include Bumphead Parrotfish and Humphead Wrasse, the former often seen in small groups that are happy to approach divers.

While suitable for divers of all abilities, it is likely to take a number of dives to appreciate everything that Ave Maria has to offer. The combination of healthy coral reef, prolific fish life, impressive granite formations and the chance to encounter pelagics, makes this site one not to miss.

Booby Rock

- Reef type: Granitic
- Level: Intermediate
- Depth: 12 – 20 m
  (40 – 65 ft)
- Snorkelling: no
- Rating: ★★★★

A school of Orbicular Batfish at Booby Rock.

Booby Rock is located to the north of Praslin, a 20-minute boat ride from Anse Volbert. Its granite slopes rise from the water and are crowned in lush green vegetation. Beneath the surface the rocks tumble down to a depth of around 20 m (65 ft) and a one-hour dive is the perfect amount of time to circle the entire island. Depending on the time of year, the journey to Booby Rock can be a little choppy but keep an eye open for dolphins, which regularly pass by. The exposed location of the site means that the current can often be strong and will also dictate the direction of the dive.

The coral reef of Booby Rock consists of the typical granite boulders, that are covered in sponges and encrusting corals. Branching and table *Acropora* spp. corals cling onto the rocks and are surrounded by clouds of Indian Dascyllus, while within the branching colonies of *Pocillopora* spp., Freckled Hawkfish and Rust-spotted Guard Crabs wait for their prey.

Booby Rock is one of the best locations in the area for Whitetip Reef Shark encounters, and it is not unusual to see several sharks on a dive. These inquisitive sharks have a characteristic white tip on the dorsal fin and tail. They are harmless unless provoked and will often circle divers before disappearing out of view. Spotted Eagle Rays are also frequent visitors and squadrons of a dozen or more rays regularly glide above the reef.

Aside from the customary Seychelles reef inhabitants, Booby Rock is renowned for its school of Bumphead Parrotfish. Groups of three or four of these gigantic fish are commonly observed feeding on the reef, though on occasion the entire school comes together and can number over 20 individuals.

On account of its isolation, Booby Rock is regularly visited by larger marine species, which come to the island to hunt in the shallows around the granite reef. Sailfish and dolphins are often spotted from the dive boat and occasionally encountered under the waves.

Channel Rock

- Reef type: Granitic
- Level: Advanced
- Depth: 10 – 25 m
  (33 – 80 ft)
- Snorkelling: no
- Rating: ★★★★

The boulders at Channel Rock are swathed in orange sponges.

Located to the east of Praslin Island, halfway to La Digue, is a submerged granite reef known as Channel Rock. At low tide the pinnacle of the tallest boulder just breaks the surface of the ocean, but for much of the time the reef is hidden beneath the waves. This site can be dived from centres located both on Praslin and La Digue. Owing to its depth, and the fact that it can be subjected to strong currents, Channel Rock is only suitable for advanced divers.

The seabed lies at a depth of 20 – 25 m (65 – 80 ft) and the sandy substrate is broken up by a series of large, sponge-encrusted, granite boulders. These are spaced out sufficiently as to require a swim of a short distance between each section of the reef. In addition to the numerous smaller boulders dotted towards the edge of the site, a large granite formation dominates the centre and contains numerous channels and ledges, which provide shelter to an array of marine life including mesmerizing octopuses.

Coral cover at this site is limited to widely spaced colonies of branching *Pocillopora* spp.

and instead encrusting sponges and stunted *Tubastrea* spp. corals dominate the landscape, covering every inch of the granite structures. The fish life at Channel Rock is impressive however, with plenty of butterflyfish and chromis. Like many of the offshore sites within the inner islands, schools of bright yellow snapper hover above the reef, with thousands of densely packed individuals providing excellent photographic opportunities.

The strong currents that wash over the site also bring with them the chance to see larger reef inhabitants such as stingrays, Whitetip Reef Sharks and barracuda. Hawksbill Turtles are frequent visitors and feed on the sponges that carpet the granite boulders.

Coral Garden

- Reef type: Carbonate
- Level: Beginner
- Depth: 8 – 16 m
  (26 – 52 ft)
- Snorkelling: yes
- Rating: ★★★

Delicate *Echinopora lamellosa* corals adorn the reef at Coral Garden.

Located halfway between Praslin and Curieuse Islands and situated within the Curieuse Marine National Park, Coral Garden is a short distance from Côte d'Or. A carbonate reef with a maximum depth of 16 m (52 ft), this dive site has an abundance of reef fish. Visibility ranges from 5 – 20 m (15 – 65 ft) and with plenty of small critters to be discovered, this is a popular site with macro enthusiasts.

Coral Garden has many species of reef fish typical to Seychelles, as well as some less common examples. Both the Arabian Butterflyfish (*Chaetodon melapterus*) and the Somali Butterflyfish (*Chaetodon leucopleura*), absent on most reefs within the inner islands, have been spotted at this site. Amidst the *Acropora* spp. thickets, African Pygmy Angelfish flash their orange-and-blue livery, while schools of yellow snapper sway with the current.

Aside from the abundant reef fish, Coral Garden has multifarious macro subjects making it an ideal site for photographers. Peacock Groupers lie motionless under the corals and many are attended by tiny wrasse and cleaner shrimp, which go about their business removing parasites and attending to wounds. A variety of nudibranch species can also be found on the reef and it is not unusual to see a number of species on a single dive.

At night the array of marine creatures changes as crabs and lobsters exit their daytime hideaways and Moorish Idols transform into their evening wear becoming a darker colour. Look out for parrotfish wedged into the reef, encased in their mucous bubbles.

Nudibranchs such as *Goniobranchus albopunctatus* are one of the macro species that can be found at Coral Garden.

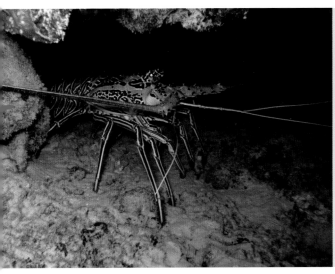

Point Rouge

- Reef type: Granitic
- Level: Intermediate
- Depth: 10 – 20 m
  (33 – 65 ft)
- Snorkelling: no
- Rating: ★★★

Painted Lobsters can be found hiding under the rocks at Point Rouge.

Point Rouge is situated at the southernmost tip of Curieuse Island, within the Curieuse Marine National Park, and is so called because of the large red granite rocks that protrude from the point of the island. The site is visited by dive centres located on Anse Volbert and is a 10-minute boat journey from the beach. Maximum depth is around 20 m (65 ft) and currents can often be strong, making Point Rouge a site for more experienced divers.

Although there are few large coral colonies, in places the substrate is covered with a carpet of pink and purple soft corals. Reef fish include inquisitive cowfish, sullen-looking Peacock Groupers and bright blue Palette Surgeonfish. Jacks are particularly common and large schools often visit the reef, where they can be seen swirling around rock formations, pursuing glassfish as they pass. Jobfish often join the mêlée, preferring to pick off fish that have become disoriented in the water column.

Point Rouge is a popular site for seeing rays; Spotted Eagle Rays regularly fly in formation above the reef. One of their cousins, the Mobula

Ray, is a regular visitor and on occasion schools of over 30 individuals swim through the site.

The exposed nature of the location means Point Rouge offers the prospect of seeing larger species rarely observed at other sites. Guitar Sharks are found throughout the inner islands but sightings are uncommon. The waters around Curieuse Island, and in particular Point Rouge, offer some of the best opportunities to see these amazing creatures. There have even been sightings of Hammerhead Sharks, although these encounters are infrequent.

The inquisitive Peacock Grouper.

St Pierre

- Reef type: Granitic
- Level: Beginner
- Depth: 8 – 12 m
  (26 – 40 ft)
- Snorkelling: yes
- Rating: ★★★

The distinctive island of St Pierre rises out of the ocean.

The tiny island of St Pierre lies approximately 1.5 km (1 mile) off the coast of Praslin in the bay of Côte d'Or. It is uninhabited, populated only by a few coconut palms and nesting seabirds. The waters surrounding St Pierre are part of the Curieuse Marine National Park. Only a five-minute boat journey from the dive centres located on the Anse Volbert beach, this site is popular with both divers and snorkellers. Frequently used by local dive centres for introductory dives and training sessions, the maximum depth of the site is around 12 m (40 ft).

The St Pierre site consists of granite boulders covered in coral, predominantly from the *Acropora* genus. There is plenty of fish life with Striped Surgeonfish and bristletooths rushing between coral colonies. Like many of Praslin's sites, Whitetip Reef Sharks are regularly encountered and spend much of the daylight hours hiding under ledges and boulders. Away from the reef, schools of fusiliers swirl in the water column where they are joined by Spotted Eagle Rays flying in formation.

St Pierre is a shallow dive, which rarely experiences strong current and is perfect for taking your time and searching for the smaller reef inhabitants. Make sure to look out for stonefish, which blend into the substrate waiting to ambush their unsuspecting prey. Whip corals are also great places to look for macro subjects with gobies and commensal shrimp making them their homes.

The reef around St Pierre is ideal for divers of all abilities and is also an excellent location for night dives. At night numerous species hidden during the day, become active as they search for food. Various crabs and shrimps can be seen along with the giant Spanish Dancer nudibranch, while Whitetip Reef Sharks come out from their daytime hiding places in search of an evening meal.

South Marianne Island

- Reef type: Granitic
- Level: Intermediate
- Depth: 14 – 25 m
  (46 – 80 ft)
- Snorkelling: no
- Rating: ★★★★★

Grey Reef Sharks are the highlight of any dive at South Marianne Island.

Marianne is a small granitic island located almost 10 km (6 miles) from La Digue and around 19 km (12 miles) from Praslin. It can be dived with operators on both Praslin Island and La Digue when conditions are calm enough, and is certainly well worth the distance involved.

As the name suggests, the dive site is located at the southern tip of the island. The currents are sometimes strong here, making it more suitable for intermediate to advanced divers. The seabed lies at around 25 m (80 ft) and the dive progresses in a single direction depending on the current. Below the surface granite pinnacles rise from the sandy substrate forming cathedral-like structures and creating precipitous ravines and narrow gulleys. The coral is confined to the granite formations with a sandy, rubble bottom in between. It is not the coral, however, that brings divers to this site but the chance to see sharks and pelagic fish in abundance.

Large schools of jacks, tuna and barracuda often visit, brought in by the strong currents that rush over the granite formations. Hawksbill Turtles can also be seen casually swimming past. South Marianne is unique in that several species of shark can be seen in one dive. Whitetip Reef Sharks are frequently observed as are sleeping Nurse Sharks, wedged into crevices in the rock and surrounded by schools of thousands of glassfish. Occasional visitors include Blacktip Reef Sharks and Shark Rays, but the real stars of the show are the Grey Reef Sharks.

South Marianne is famous for its aggregation of Grey Reef Sharks, which patrol the submerged granite boulders. It is not unusual to see several individuals but at times over 30 sharks have been encountered. Though the larger aggregations are perhaps not as common as they once were, South Marianne still offers a fantastic opportunity to get up close to these magnificent creatures.

The dramatic underwater landscape of granite formations makes South Marianne worthy of a visit alone. Add to that, incredible fish life, plentiful pelagics and the chance to see a good number of sharks and it is no wonder that this is one of the premier dive sites within the inner islands.

Silhouette and North Island

Anse Mondon

- Reef type: Granitic
- Level: Beginner
- Depth: 5 – 14 m
  (16 – 46 ft)
- Snorkelling: yes
- Rating: ★★★

Porcelain Crabs at Anse Mondon make a great macro photography subject.

Anse Mondon is located in a small, protected bay to the north of Silhouette Island. It is a rocky reef, which slopes down to a depth of 14 m (46 ft). This is a shallow and easy dive but that is not to say there is nothing to see, as marine life is plentiful. The reef has a good diversity of butterflyfish and angelfish as well as many small reef fish, which hover above the coral heads in their thousands.

The rocks at Anse Mondon are covered in algae and soft coral, making it the perfect habitat to search for nudibranchs and other macro subjects. Several species of nudibranch uncommon elsewhere within the inner islands have been found here, as well as more common species, such as the Spanish Dancer.

Other macro subjects include Devil Scorpionfish and Porcelain Crabs, which cling to their anemone hosts. They share them with Seychelles Anemonefish or Skunk Anemonefish, or with both

on some occasions. At the bottom of the reef, Fire Dartfish hover above their sandy burrows, always on the lookout in a state of perpetual nervousness. These beautiful little fish dive into their burrows at the first sign of danger, but with a little patience and a slow advance, it is possible to approach them closely.

It is not just the macro life at Anse Mondon that is a draw; Thorny Rays are regularly spotted feeding in a cloud of sand and Hawksbill Turtles are sometimes found resting on the rocks or lazily swimming above the reef.

With the reef slope starting at a depth of 5 m (16 ft), it is possible to finish the safety stop while continuing to search the reef for marine life. Anse Mondon is perfect for beginner divers, snorkellers and underwater photographers due to its shallow depth and lack of currents.

Grande Barbe

- Reef type: Granitic
- Level: Intermediate
- Depth: 12 – 26 m
  (40 – 85 ft)
- Snorkelling: no
- Rating: ★★★★

The beach at Grande Barbe is important for nesting Hawksbill Turtles.

This dive site takes its name from the Grande Barbe plateau, located on the north-west coast of Silhouette Island. An area of outstanding natural beauty, the plateau lies in the shadow of Seychelles' second highest peak, Mount Dauban, and has an important Hawksbill Turtle nesting beach as well as extensive mangrove wetlands.

At the southern end of the beach the white sand gives way to a granite headland, which rises steeply above the waves. Underwater the granite boulders drop down to a sandy substrate at a depth of approximately 26 m (85 ft). Coral cover is sparse at this site, with small sporadic colonies hanging onto the surface of the granite. The rock formations are impressive, with numerous giant boulders providing a seascape of intricate swim-throughs and passages. What Grande Barbe lacks in coral it more than makes up for in fish life with every overhang and ledge home to numerous sweetlips and good sized groupers.

Whitetip Reef Sharks are a common sight resting on the sand, while Nurse and Grey Reef Sharks are also frequently encountered. As would be expected for a site adjacent to an important turtle nesting beach, Hawksbill Turtles are numerous. Grande Barbe is also an excellent site to see Humphead Wrasse and Bumphead Parrotfish.

A dive here usually finishes in the shallows amongst the granite boulders where wrasse dart above the reef. Away from the shore, large schools of batfish and occasionally Devil Rays move in synchronized formation.

As with all dive sites around Silhouette, Grande Barbe can be accessed by liveaboard or through the Eco Centre based near the Hilton Labriz hotel on the island. Grande Barbe is not a site for coral enthusiasts or lovers of macro photography, but will certainly deliver for those seeking encounters with pelagics or the larger reef inhabitants.

Sprat City

- Reef type: Carbonate
- Level: Beginner
- Depth: 7 – 24 m
  (23 – 78 ft)
- Snorkelling: no
- Rating: ★★★★
-

Glassfish swirl around a coral head at Sprat City.

North Island is 5 km (3 miles) north of Silhouette. The private island is home to a luxury resort, labelled as one of the world's most exclusive retreats. Located on the west coast of North Island is the dive site known as Sprat City. This coral reef can be dived either from the resort's in-house dive centre on North Island or from the dive centre on Silhouette Island.

Sprat City is a deep carbonate reef dropping to around 24 m (78 ft) depth, formed of a series of coral pinnacles separated by sandy channels. Coral diversity is excellent with large colonies of *Porites* spp. interspersed with thickets of *Acropora* spp. Reef fish are plentiful here, with the usual cast of butterflyfish and angelfish that are found around the other inner islands. Other species to look out for include scorpionfish, lionfish and the ubiquitous batfish. Small groups of Bumphead Parrotfish are frequently encountered, as are Marbled Rays as they glide across the reef.

The site is usually dived at times of the year when sea conditions are calm making it suitable for all

levels of diver. A dive at Sprat City often starts at one of the shallower pinnacles and progresses across the sand from one coral area to another. It is the Whitetip Reef Sharks that Sprat City is perhaps best known for, with several individuals often found grouped together resting on the seabed. The sharks are usually quite tolerant and will allow divers to approach to within a couple of metres (six feet) before swimming away. The Whitetip Reef Sharks are a constant feature of the dive site, often appearing out of the blue to circle divers before disappearing again.

Although North Island has a number of excellent accessible sites, with its healthy coral, diversity of reef fish and numerous reef sharks, Sprat City is the one dive site not to be missed.

Glacis

⑥ Anse Etoile

Beau Vallon
③

Bel Ombre

Bel Air ● Victoria
Mont Fleuri ●

②

④ ● Port Launay

● Port Glaud

Les Mamelles ●

Cascade ●

Grand Anse ●

MAHÉ

Pointe la Rue ●

Anse Aux Pins ●

Anse Boileau ●

Au Cap ●

Indian Ocean

Anse à la Mouche ●   Anse Royale ●
①

● Baie Lazare

Takamaka ●

SAINTE
ANNE

⑤

CERF

NORTH
ISLAND

PRASLIN
LA
DIGUE

SILHOUETTE
ISLAND

SEYCHELLES

MAHÉ

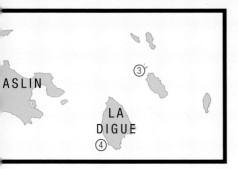

Guide to Snorkel Spots

There are numerous shallow reefs and lagoons in the inner islands of Seychelles that offer excellent conditions for snorkelling. This chapter includes some of the most popular snorkelling spots but there are many more that can be explored.

Key to highlights at each site

Shark	
Turtle	
Macro (i.e small creatures)	
Schools of fish	
Ray	
Coral	
Soft coral	
Wreck	

KEY TO SNORKEL SPOTS

Mahé
1. Anse Royale
2. Baie Ternay Marine National Park
3. Fishermen's Cove
4. Port Launay Marine National Park
5. Sainte Anne Marine National Park
6. Sunset Beach

Praslin & surrounding islands
1. Anse Lazio
2. Curieuse Marine National Park
3. Iles Cocos Marine National Park
4. Anse Source D'Argent

Map showing location of snorkel spots.

Mahé

Anse Royale

- Reef type: Granitic/ Carbonate
- Ability level: Beginner
- Depth: 1 – 3 m (3 – 10 ft)
- Rating: ★★★
- Accessibility: By road
- Facilities: Car park, shop, restaurant/café

Looking out to Ile Souris from Anse Royale beach.

On the south-east coast of Mahé Island, Anse Royale is a charming beach dotted with granite boulders, creating a series of small, private coves that are sheltered by large Takamaka trees.

This snorkel spot is best visited during the north-west monsoon and provides a good alternative if areas on the west side of the island are too rough. The coral reef is great for beginners as it starts close to the beach. It is also protected from the majority of wave action by the reef crest that is a short distance from shore. Close to the shoreline the water is shallow, only 0.5 – 1 m (1½ – 3 ft) deep, with lush seagrass beds and gardens of *Turbinaria* spp. algae. Plenty of marine life can be seen with moray eels hunting in the open, large schools of rabbitfish darting across the seabed and stingrays feeding in the seagrass.

You should enter the water in front of the small car park on the northern side of the bay. Swim out following the granite rocks on your left, towards the small island called Ile Souris. The reef here comprises massive *Porites* spp. corals dotted between seagrass and sand. Once you reach the granite boulders of Ile Souris, the amount of marine life increases with many species found, including butterflyfish, goatfish and parrotfish. as well as the smaller marine creatures, such as nudibranchs, which hide in the bright green turtle grass algae. The water becomes a little deeper by the island but still remains shallower than 2 m (6 ft) until you reach the reef crest. It is not recommended to swim past the island unless you are a confident snorkeller, as strong currents can sweep around the island out to sea, making swimming back to shore difficult.

Accessibility is straightforward, as the beach and small car park are adjacent to the main road. It is best to visit at low tide, as there is a limited amount of beach available at high tide. The centre of Anse Royale, which has several restaurants and shops, is further down the beach.

Baie Ternay Marine National Park

- Reef type: Carbonate
- Ability level: Beginner
- Depth: 4 – 18 m (13 – 60 ft)
- Rating: ★★★★★
- Accessibility: By boat
- Facilities: None

Baie Ternay Marine National Park.

The Baie Ternay Marine National Park is not only an excellent dive site (see page 50), it is also one of the best locations for snorkelling on Mahé. Snorkel excursions are regularly offered by tour operators on Mahé. A variety of tours are available on all sizes of boat; some offer a whole day with a BBQ lunch and some a shorter snorkelling trip.

There are many areas to snorkel within Baie Ternay although the most commonly visited spot is the reef in the middle of the bay. The coral reef of Baie Ternay begins at a shallow depth, which can even be exposed at low tide, at the edge of large seagrass beds. The shallow area of the reef offers fantastic snorkelling for beginners with small coral bommies spread across the sand. These bommies shelter juvenile reef fish, small moray eels and the occasional turtle. Further out from the shore the coral reef slopes down slowly to around 16 m (52 ft). More experienced snorkellers may wish to venture a little further to explore this deeper reef where Green and Hawksbill Turtles, eagle rays and even the occasional Whitetip Reef Shark can be seen.

As well as the central reef, there are also excellent coral reefs on both sides of the bay. In front of the small beach, known as Anse du Riz or Secret Beach, on the northerly side of the bay there is a beautiful carbonate reef that extends onto the granite rocks on the shoreline. This complex reef starts at around 0.5 m (1½ ft) and drops to around 14 m (46 ft) at its deepest point. Anse du Riz's main 'secret' is a brackish pool behind the beach, which is fantastic to explore and great for a quick snorkel amongst the mangroves.

If visiting by catamaran there are mooring buoys available within the marine park. This is a good spot to moor overnight, and means you are in the perfect location for an early morning snorkel. Note that a marine park fee must be paid.

Baie Ternay is exposed to the effects of the north-west monsoon (November – March) and snorkelling is often not possible at this time of year due to the rough sea conditions. Also be aware of boat traffic when snorkelling in Baie Ternay as it can get busy with many snorkel and dive boats visiting.

Fishermen's Cove

- Reef type: Carbonate
- Ability level: Beginner
- Depth: 1 – 5 m (3 – 16 ft)
- Rating: ★★★
- Accessibility: By foot
- Facilities: Car park, restaurant/café, toilets, lifeguard, shop
-

The western end of Beau Vallon beach with the Fishermen's Cove hotel in the distance.

On the westerly side of Beau Vallon beach, there is a coral reef directly in front of Le Meridien Fishermen's Cove hotel. This snorkel spot is easily accessed from the popular Beau Vallon beach, and offers a perfect 'walk in' reef for beginner snorkellers. If you are staying in Beau Vallon, this reef is close by and is a great place to practise snorkelling.

You should enter the ocean just in front of the small stream that runs into the sea by the side of the hotel, as this is in line with the edge of the reef. Caution should be taken when entering at low tide as there can be urchins in the seagrass in front of the reef. If entering the water here, follow the edge of the reef around to the left, heading towards the granite rocks on the shoreline. Be careful not to swim too far along the coastline as it can be a long swim back, especially if there is a slight current. Also be aware of fast-moving jet skis that frequently race around Beau Vallon bay.

The reef at Fishermen's Cove begins at around 0.5 – 1 m (1½ – 3 ft) depth and slowly slopes down to around 4 m (13 ft). Small branching corals dominate the reef and are home to a variety of reef fishes. Damselfish, parrotfish, rabbitfish and vividly coloured wrasse are all found in good numbers. Large schools of surgeonfish graze the algae on the reef like flocks of birds, and a resident Hawksbill Turtle can often be seen slowly swimming across the reef.

Unfortunately Fishermen's Cove is not accessible all year round, as during the north-west monsoon (November – March) the sea can be rough making snorkelling here impossible.

If driving to the site, you can park in the Berjaya Hotel car park, then walk to the beach through the hotel. Turn left when you get to the beach and walk for around 200 m (650 ft) until you reach the start of the reef. It is recommended that you leave any valuables in your car rather than unattended on the beach.

Port Launay Marine National Park

- Reef type: Granitic/Carbonate
- Ability level: Beginner
- Depth: 1 – 9 m (3 – 30 ft)
- Rating: ★★★★
- Accessibility: By road
- Facilities: Car park, restaurant/café, toilets, shop

The sheltered bay of Port Launay is excellent for snorkelling all year round.

The Port Launay Marine National Park offers a wonderful snorkelling experience for all abilities. The bay is sheltered making its inviting waters relatively calm all year round.

Port Launay has the fantastic advantage that the coral reef is accessible straight from the beach. For beginner snorkellers the water is shallow enough that you can stand up, although be careful not to stand on any coral or marine life. There is a carbonate reef on both the left and righthand side of the bay with a sandy channel in the middle. Be sure to stick to the sides of the bay as there are often a number of boats in the middle of the channel, which is designated as a no swimming area. It is important to remain alert for boat traffic and to stay together as a group.

Close to shore you will find isolated coral bommies and dense patches of algae. The visibility in this shallow area can be limited but if you feel confident to swim out of your depth, snorkel a little further out from shore and the visibility should improve. On the lefthand side of the bay you can head towards the large cross on top of the granite rocks. Just past these rocks the reef widens and drops to around 9 m (30 ft) in depth. There are a number of huge coral formations here, some nearly 5 m (16 ft) in diameter. The reef also extends onto the granite rocks and there are some beautiful underwater rock formations. There is a good amount of fish life here, with the occasional Green Turtle and eagle ray seen swimming by. Be aware of how far out you have swum and never snorkel past the mouth of the bay, as there can be strong currents.

The reef on the righthand side follows a similar structure to that of the left. Head out with the granite rocks on the shoreline to your right. As with the reef on the lefthand side, further out from shore the visibility increases and the reef widens.

There is parking available right next to the beach, although at weekends this can get rather crowded. Bordering the beach is the Constance Ephelia hotel, which has several restaurants and bathroom facilities. There is also a small shop a five-minute walk south from Port Launay beach, where you can buy drinks and snacks.

Sainte Anne Marine National Park

- Reef type: Granitic/ Carbonate
- Ability level: Beginner
- Depth: 1 – 8 m (3 – 26 ft)
- Rating: ★★★
- Accessibility: By boat
- Facilities: None

Sainte Anne offers many good snorkelling opportunities.

Sainte Anne was the first area in Seychelles to be declared a Marine National Park in 1973. Situated 5 km (3 miles) off the coast of Mahé, the marine park covers an area of 15 sq km (6 sq miles) and includes six islands – Sainte Anne, Moyenne, Round, Long, Cachee and Cerf Islands.

Sainte Anne's close proximity to Victoria makes it a popular choice for snorkelling trips. Access to the marine park is by boat from Victoria, unless you are staying at a resort on one of the islands within the park. There are daily boat tours to Sainte Anne from Mahé organized by local tour operators. These are often a half day or full day trip, and usually include snorkelling and a visit to Cerf, Round or Moyenne Island for lunch.

Due to its size and geographical features, a variety of marine habitats can be seen within the marine park; seagrass beds, sand flats, patch carbonate reefs and granite reefs are all found here. There are extensive seagrass beds that are one of the largest in the inner islands and the park also contains important turtle nesting beaches.

There are numerous snorkelling opportunities within the park at the various islands. One of the best spots is in the channel between Moyenne and Ste Anne Island. You can also go ashore on Moyenne Island to meet some of the Giant Tortoises that live there. If you are visiting Cerf Island there is also some first-class snorkelling in front of the island, facing Mahé.

The seagrass beds and coral reefs support an abundance of marine life. Green and Hawksbill Turtles are fairly common and eagle rays swim slowly past. The corals are in recovery following mass coral mortality after the 1998 El Niño bleaching event, however there are still some healthy areas with extensive *Echinopora* spp. and *Turbinaria* spp. colonies present. Many reef fishes are found here and you might see small shoals of squid swimming in the water column. Their distinctive swimming motion and ability to rapidly change colour make them quite a spectacle.

As with all marine national parks in Seychelles, fishing and motorized watersports are prohibited, as is the collection of shells and coral.

Sunset Beach

- Reef type: Granitic/Carbonate
- Ability level: Intermediate
- Depth: > 8 m (26 ft)
- Rating: ★★★★
- Accessibility: By road
- Facilities: Car park, restaurant/café, toilets
-

Sunset Beach with the hotel in the distance.

Sunset Beach is close to Beau Vallon and is perfect for a short snorkel if you are spending the day at the beach. Situated next to the Sunset Beach hotel in Glacis on the north-west coast of Mahé, this snorkel spot is suitable for intermediate to advanced snorkellers. The hotel is in a small, secluded cove with a pretty beach. Access to the beach through the hotel is restricted to their guests, but a semi-paved path located 40 m (130 ft) north of the hotel entrance provides a means of entry for the public.

The best snorkelling in this cove is on the lefthand side of the bay. Enter the water close to the rocks on the lefthand side of the beach and follow them around to the point of the cove. Under the hotel bar large schools of Sergeant Majors and diamondfish swirl around you, and corals hug the rocks. Snorkelling further out of the cove around the point you will see that the reef descends from the rocks into a large carbonate reef. The depth drops off quite quickly here to around 6 m (20 ft) so this is suitable for more advanced snorkellers. A small group of Bumphead Parrotfish is occasionally seen here, along with small eagle rays.

Sunset Beach is affected by the north-west monsoon and large waves breaking on the beach can make it difficult to enter the water. Even when the water is fairly calm, there can be a strong undertow and caution is advised.

If arriving at Sunset Beach by car you will need to find parking near to the hotel, as the hotel car park is for their resident guests only. There is usually space to park by the bus stop on the opposite side of the road to the hotel, or further along the coastal road.

Schools of damselfish congregate below the hotel restaurant.

Praslin and surrounding islands

Anse Lazio

- Reef type: Granitic
- Ability level: Beginner
- Depth: 1 – 5 m
  (3 – 16 ft)
- Rating: ★★★
- Accessibility: On foot
- Facilities: Car park,
  restaurant/café, toilets,
  lifeguard

Repeatedly voted one of the best beaches in the world, a visit to Anse Lazio is a must on any trip to Seychelles.

Perhaps the most photographed beach on Praslin, Anse Lazio is one of the prettiest beaches in Seychelles. With its crystal blue water, sparkling white sand and extraordinary surrounding landscape, it is certainly not to be missed. As well as its natural beauty, Anse Lazio also boasts some terrific snorkelling.

Parking is limited at Anse Lazio so if you are driving, try to get there early to ensure there is space available. Alternatively you can take the public bus and walk from the main road to the beach (around 10 – 15 minutes), or join one of the tours that visit the beach (often organized as a day trip along with the Vallée de Mai). There are a couple of small restaurants at the beach, which also have toilet facilities. You will need to bring your own snorkel equipment, as you will be unable to hire any at the beach. As with any of the beaches in Seychelles, it is not advisable to leave any valuables unattended.

The middle of the bay is mainly sand therefore it is best to snorkel on the rocks at either end of the beach. A range of corals can be found on the granite boulders with colourful reef fishes darting in and out with the movement of the current. Hawksbill Turtles, eagle rays and even reef sharks can be seen here. Take care not to be carried by the surge of the waves onto the rocks and do not swim around either point as there can be strong currents.

While there is usually a lifeguard on site, in the north-west monsoon this beach can be subjected to big waves and is not suitable for snorkelling. Make sure you check the sea conditions before making the trip there.

Curieuse Marine National Park

- Reef type: Carbonate/ Granitic
- Ability level: Beginner
- Depth: 1 – 5 m (3 – 16 ft)
- Rating: ★★★
- Accessibility: By boat
- Facilities: Toilets

Aldabra Giant Tortoises roam freely on Curieuse Island.

Perhaps better known for its population of Aldabra Giant Tortoises and the ruins of a former leper colony, the Curieuse Marine National Park also offers some great snorkelling for all abilities making it an ideal day excursion from Praslin.

Curieuse Island lies 2 km (1¼ miles) from Praslin and can only be reached by boat. It is one of the larger islands within the inner islands and home to over 100 reintroduced Aldabra Giant Tortoises. The beaches are important sites for nesting Hawksbill Turtles while the hills and valleys are home to the endemic Coco de Mer Palm.

Curieuse can be visited through an organized day trip with one of the local tour operators or by hiring a boat taxi from Anse Volbert on Praslin. These trips will usually take you to Baie Laraie and the Doctor's House at Anse José, which has been converted into a small museum detailing the history of the island. At the Doctor's House there are toilets but no café or restaurant. If you visit as part of an organized tour, lunch is usually included. Curieuse can only be visited for the day, as there are no hotels or guesthouses.

The best snorkelling spot is in front of the Doctor's House. Enter the water in front of the house where the beach slopes away to seagrass beds. Swim out for around 20 m (65 ft) and you will find granite rocks scattered on the sea floor, accompanied by plenty of reef fishes. The seagrass beds also contain a wealth of marine life including puffer and porcupinefish, grazing Green Turtles and juvenile reef fishes hiding in amongst the blades of seagrass.

Stingrays are particularly common in the sandy area at the southern end of the beach, and if you continue to snorkel east, the shoreline transforms from beach to granite rocks. These rocks create interesting underwater formations and shrimps and lobsters can be found hiding in their crevices.

At certain times of the year the beach at Anse Jose can become busy with a number of visiting boats. It is important to be aware of boat traffic when snorkelling and remain close to the shoreline. Currents can be strong on occasion so be sure to remain in shallow water unless you are a confident swimmer.

Iles Cocos Marine National Park

- Reef type: Granitic
- Ability level: Beginner
- Depth: 1 – 5 m
  (3 – 16 ft)
- Rating: ★★★★
- Accessibility: By boat
- Facilities: None
-

Large schools of surgeonfish graze on algae at Iles Cocos.

Famed for its friendly Hawksbill Turtles and regarded as one of the best spots in Seychelles for snorkelling, Iles Cocos is a small Marine National Park 7 km (4 miles) north of La Digue. The marine park comprises three small, uninhabited granite islets; Ile Cocos, Ile La Fouche and Ilot Plate. Ile Cocos can only be accessed by boat, and as there are not any hotels on the island, only day visits can be made. Many local tour operators offer trips to Ile Cocos from Praslin and La Digue, and your hotel or guesthouse should be able to advise you on these.

Between the granite islets there is a shallow reef area, which has a maximum depth of around 3 m (10 ft), and this is the typical snorkelling spot. The shallow depth makes it ideal for beginner snorkellers. The carbonate reef here is in recovery as it suffered significant coral mortality after the El Niño event in 1998. The rubble reef is now slowly rejuvenating and is smothered in small *Acropora* spp. and *Pocillopora* spp. corals. Schools of grazing surgeonfish and brilliantly coloured parrotfish swim across the reef, whilst big-eyed soldierfish drift motionless above.

The main attraction, however, is the encountering of friendly Hawksbill Turtles. They can be seen at many of the snorkel spots in Seychelles but here they seem to be relatively unafraid of people and are happy to be approached. This can allow you to have an up-close-and-personal encounter with one of the world's oldest reptiles, an experience not to be forgotten! Despite the close proximity of these turtles, please do not attempt to touch or feed them.

Ile Cocos is famed for its friendly Hawksbill Turtles.

Anse Source D'Argent

- Reef type: Carbonate
- Ability level: Beginner
- Depth: 1 – 3 m (3 – 10 ft)
- Rating: ★★★
- Accessibility: On foot
- Facilities: Restaurant/ café
-

The stunning beach at Anse Source D'Argent.

Anse Source D'Argent is located on the south-west coast of La Digue Island. Consistently voted as one of the most beautiful beaches in the world, the powder white sand and granite boulders feature frequently in advertising campaigns promoting the ultimate paradise destination.

Access to the beach is through the entrance to Union Estate, for which there is an entry fee (SCR100 at the time of going to print). Within the estate there is a traditional coconut mill and copra factory as well as a vanilla plantation and an old traditional plantation house. There is an enclosure, which is home to several Aldabra Giant Tortoises and a handful of stalls selling vanilla and local souvenirs. The estate can be reached by bicycle, taxi or ox-and-cart. Bicycles can be left near the restaurant where the beach path begins, and the rest of the journey must then be undertaken on foot.

Although over 1 km (⅔ mile) in length, Anse Source D'Argent is actually a succession of small beaches, separated by sculpted granite boulders and accessed by a narrow, winding path. Seagrass beds run the length of the coast, intermingled with sandy areas and a rubble reef. The reef crest begins 50 m (165 ft) from shore and is often buffeted by waves. It is not advisable to swim out past this crest as the currents can be strong and the depth increases quickly.

Closer to shore the waters are calm and protected but can become extremely shallow at low tide. The best snorkelling is at high tide, when fish dart among the seagrass beds and moray eels can be seen peering out from the sporadic coral colonies found along the reef. Also during high tide Hawksbill Turtles cross the reef crest and venture closer to shore.

The shallow nature of the reef means there is no boat traffic, which makes Anse Source D'Argent the perfect location to take children for a day at the beach and a glimpse of Seychelles' magical underwater world.

Marine Creature Identification

The sheer diversity of animals in the underwater world can be confusing to those unfamiliar with the marine environment. This section aims to assist the reader in identifying and understanding some of the marine creatures found in Seychelles. Not all species that have been recorded in Seychelles are featured in this guide, as it concentrates on those that are most commonly seen within the inner islands.

Dascyllus crowd around a *Pocillopora* coral.

Species are classified into different groups (known as taxa), which are based upon a hierarchical system of fixed levels called taxonomic classification. The inclusion of organisms within each taxa centres on their descent from the nearest common ancestor. In this guide we have used eight main taxonomic ranks: Kingdom, Phylum, Class, Subclass, Order, Family, Genus and Species. At the highest level a Kingdom contains a number of Phyla, which in turn comprises several Classes and so on with each rank becoming increasingly specialized until you reach the level of an individual species.

An example of a taxonomic tree for the Emperor Angelfish (*Pomacanthus imperator*) would be as follows:

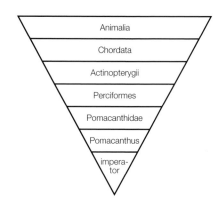

Animalia

Chordata

Actinopterygii

Perciformes

Pomacanthidae

Pomacanthus

impera-tor

The Emperor Angelfish (*Pomacanthus imperator*).

In this guide each group of marine animals or plants is separated into their various taxa and a 'quick reference index' page is located at the back of the book to assist readers in finding the relevant group section.

There is a brief explanation at the beginning of each group section, and where necessary an anatomical diagram has been provided to assist with the identification of parts of the body. A photograph of a typical specimen accompanies the description of each animal or plant within the guide, highlighting identifying characteristics. Where possible both the English common name and the two-part scientific name are included, although not all species possess a common name.

Scientific names help to avoid confusion between species, as often a species' common name will differ between localities. The scientific system of binomial nomenclature is used to provide each species with a name composed of two parts, predominantly derived from Latin. This scientific name is made up of the Genus (first word) and the Species (second word). The Genus is always capitalized and refers to a group of organisms with similar characteristics. A loose definition of a species is a group of organisms that resemble one another closely and are capable of interbreeding to produce fertile offspring. The species name is never capitalized.

In addition to a species name, the marine creature's largest recorded size is included under each photograph.

Certain species of marine animal are found in different colour forms or are capable of temporarily changing colour to assist with camouflage or in response to some environmental cue. Other species will change their appearance at different stages through their lifecycle. For simplicity, the photograph provided within the identification guide shows the most common colour form you are likely to encounter on Seychelles reefs.

In species that exhibit dissimilar male and female colouration, the sex of the specimen in the photograph is indicated in the text. Parrotfish, which change their colouration throughout their lifecycle, are particularly challenging to identify. The parrotfish lifecycle is broadly divided into three phases; the juvenile phase (jp) and two adult phases, the initial phase (ip) and the terminal phase (tp). The particular phase shown in each photograph is identified in the accompanying text.

Most of the marine animals and plants included in this identification section have been identified to species level. However, for some of the difficult groups a single photograph has been provided as an example. This is because for certain sessile invertebrates, identification is complex and beyond the scope of this book.

When trying to identify any organism underwater, it is important to take note of several characteristics. This will help you make an accurate identification once out of the water:

Size and shape Try to memorize the shape of the creature and its size. Many fish and corals are distinguished by their shape rather than their colour.

Location Study the animal/plant and establish its preferred habitat. Is it swimming high in the water column? Or hiding under corals?

Behaviour and movement Some creatures have a distinctive behaviour or movement that distinguishes them from other species, e.g. cleaner wrasse can be seen 'cleaning' other animals.

Colour This is often the first thing you notice and is useful for identification. However, many species can change colour, which can be misleading.

Phylum Rhodophyta, Chlorophyta and Ochrophyta

Brown macro algae is found in shallow reef areas where it grows on rocky substrates.

Turf algae is a filamentous and densely packed algal assemblage that creates a short mat over the substrate.

Coralline algae is a group of hard calcareous algaes.

Sargassum algae is a brown macro algae.

Marine algae

Marine algae, also known as seaweeds, are among the most ancient members of the plant kingdom. They attach themselves to the substrate using special 'holdfast' structures. These algae, however, do not have the typical leaves, seeds, tissues or flowers that are seen in some terrestrial plants. There are three main categories of algae: red algae (e.g. Coralline algae), green algae (e.g. Macro or turf algae) and brown algae (e.g. Macro algae). All these algae manufacture their own food through the process of photosynthesis and generally reproduce asexually by cell division.

Phylum Tracheophyta

Seagrass
Seagrasses are the only marine flowering plants in the coral reef ecosystem. They often grow in great numbers and represent terrestrial grass meadows. They have a complex root structure that traps sediment and secures the seabed, they also provide food and shelter for many coral reef species. There are eight species of seagrass known in Seychelles but the two most common species in the inner islands are *Thalassia hemprichii* and *Thalassodendron ciliatum*.

Phylum Porifera

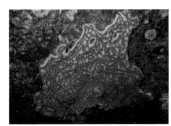

Encrusting sponge.

Ball sponge.

Irregular sponge.

Sponges
Sponges are the simplest multi-cellular animal found in the marine ecosystem. They have no true tissue layers or organs. Instead they draw in water through pores on their surface and pump it out through a large excurrent opening. Through this process the animal absorbs food and oxygen. Sponges come in a variety of shapes, colours and sizes with some less than a few centimetres in size and others several metres high.

Phylum Cnidaria

The Phylum Cnidaria includes jellyfishes, anemones, corals, sea pens, zoanthids and corallimorphs. Many cnidarian species are made up of colonies of thousands of tiny individual animals that are attached to the substrate. Others can be solitary individuals, such as anemones, or free-living like jellyfishes. When a single animal is attached to the substrate it is known as a polyp, when free swimming it is known as a medusa, as in the case of the jellyfish.

Cnidarians are radially symmetrical with cup-shaped bodies and a single opening that doubles up as the mouth and anus. Tentacles surround the opening and are used for defence or to capture prey. Within these tentacles there are small capsules called nematocysts that are used to stun their prey. Contact with some cnidarians can create a prolonged burning sensation.

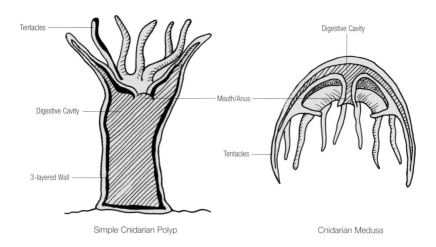

Simple Cnidarian Polyp

Cnidarian Medusa

Fire coral
Fire coral is technically not a coral, despite its name, and is more closely related to hydrozoans. Fire corals are colonial organisms that form a variety of shapes and structures. They are usually yellow to brown/orange in colour with white edging. Their surface contains thousands of translucent hairs, which can be seen clearly on most species. The hairs contain nematocysts and are capable of delivering a painful sting, which may last a few days.

Subclass Octocorallia

Octocorallia includes gorgonians, stoloniferans, soft corals and sea pens. They all have calcareous spicules within their body tissues and their polyps have eight tentacles. They are found in a variety of shapes and sizes and can be some of the most spectacular organisms encountered on a coral reef.

Gorgonians Order Gorgonacea
Common examples of gorgonians include sea fans and sea whips. They are colonial organisms that attach themselves to the substrate and often reach impressive sizes. They can be brightly coloured and are usually found in areas of strong current where they extend their polyps to capture passing nutrients.

Organ-pipe coral Order Stolonifera
Organ-pipe Coral (*Tubipora musica*) secretes a hard, red, calcium carbonate skeleton made up of a series of tubes. Within each tube is a polyp with eight feather-like tentacles, giving it the appearance of a flower. If you waft the water near the polyps, they will retract and the skeleton will be visible. Colonies of this coral tend to prefer the shallow sheltered areas of reefs.

Leather coral.

Tree corals within the family Nephtheidae are typically brightly coloured.

Xenia sp. soft coral.

Soft corals Order Alcyonacea

There are several species of soft coral found in Seychelles. Many are brightly coloured and form large tree-like structures, which attach themselves to granite boulders. They are commonly found in areas of strong current where they are able to inflate to feed. Leather corals are particularly common on shallow carbonate reefs. So-called due to their leathery appearance when the polyps are retracted, colonies of leather coral can cover large areas of reef. Flower-like Xenia corals grow in small colonies, that continuously open and close their polyps when feeding.

Subclass Hexacorallia

Included in the Hexacorallia subclass are anemones, wire corals, zoanthids, corallimorphs and hard or stony corals. All organisms in this group consist of polyps that have six tentacles or tentacles in multiples of six.

Zoanthids Order Zoanthidae

Zoanthids are typically colonial organisms, individually they are not much larger than 1 cm (⅜ in) in diameter, but together a colony can cover a large area. They feed by photosynthesis and by capturing passing plankton. Colonies can sometimes resemble certain species of coral, but can be distinguished if you waft the water adjacent to the zoanthid, which will cause the oral disc to close.

Anemones Order Actiniaria

Anemones are simple structures with an outer column and an oral disc in the centre. The disc is surrounded by numerous tentacles, which are used for defence and to capture prey. They are solitary polyps that attach themselves to the substrate. Anemones are found in a variety of colours and can range in size from a few centimetres to almost a metre in diameter.

Corallimorphs Order Corallimorpharia

Corallimorphs are simple organisms, which can be confused with anemones. In Seychelles corallimorphs are often found in colonies of several individuals, whereas anemones are solitary. Corallimorphs have a flat disc shape with a central mouth. Tentacles radiate out from the centre of the disc, like spokes.

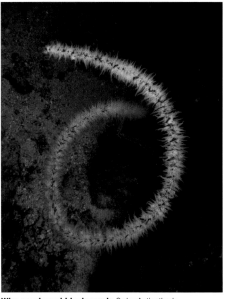

Wire corals and black corals Order Antipatharia
Wire corals are common on Seychelles reefs where they jut out from the substrate into the water column. Unlike other gorgonians, wire corals are unable to fully retract their polyps. They are found in a variety of colours including white, yellow and red and are often home to symbiotic species including gobies and shrimp. The Order Antipatharia also includes black corals.

Hard corals Order Scleractinia
Although often mistaken for plants or rocks, hard or 'hermatypic' corals are actually animals and are the living building blocks of coral reefs. The coral polyps secrete calcium carbonate to form a rigid structure called a corallite, which protects the soft polyp inside. Many polyps join together to form a coral colony. Colonies of different species of coral vary in size from a few centimetres to several metres.

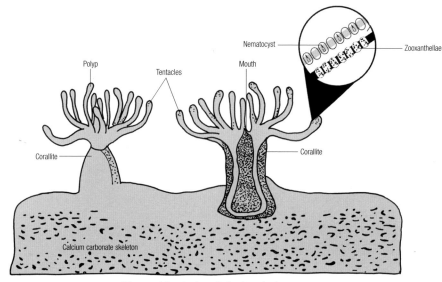

Diagram of the structure of a hard coral colony

Corals obtain their colour from the symbiotic zooxanthellae algae found within their polyps. The colour can vary within colonies of the same species, and they turn white when the corals are bleached and the zooxanthellae are expelled.

While some species of coral can be easily identified, there are many species that are similar in appearance and can therefore be confused with each other. Even individual species can be found in multiple growth forms depending on their geographic distribution, location on the reef and the environmental conditions. Furthermore, the area of coral taxonomy is constantly undergoing revision and species are likely to be re-classified in the future. With this in mind not all corals in this guide have been identified to species level, and for most user's purposes identification to life-form is sufficient.

Corals are often divided into 'life-forms' or 'growth-forms' to assist with identification. These descriptive terms are used to group corals together, with groups containing species from numerous genera. It is important to note that due to environmental conditions, some species can take on different growth forms. While the name of each type of life-form can vary depending on the identification guide used, they tend to fall into one of the following groups:

Massive (MA) Colonies are solid with roughly similar dimensions in all directions. Domed or mound shaped.

Submassive (SM) Colonies take on a columnar appearance with thick, stubby, irregular columns.

Encrusting (EN) Colonies form a thin plate that follows the contours of the substrate underneath.

Branching (BR) Colonies are tree-like and have secondary branches (branches that come off the first branch).

Digitate (D) Colonies have finger-like projections like an upturned hand. Do not have secondary branches like the branching life-form.

Tabulate (TA) Only applicable to corals in the Acropora genus, colonies form flat, table-like structures with a single attachment point in the centre of the coral.

Foliose/Plate (FO) Colonies grow into thin plates that can form tiers, whorls or vases in multiple layers. When plates grow vertically they are described as foliose, as they look like leaves.

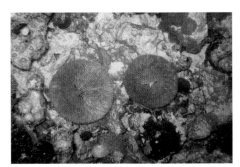

Mushroom (MU) Only applicable to corals in the Fungidae family, colonies are usually free-living and unattached to the substrate. Many have the appearance of mushrooms.

For those who wish to take their coral identification further, included within this guide are some of the most common coral species that are likely to be encountered around the inner islands of Seychelles.

At the end of the description of each coral its life-form is indicated, as shown in the photographs above and the illustration below.

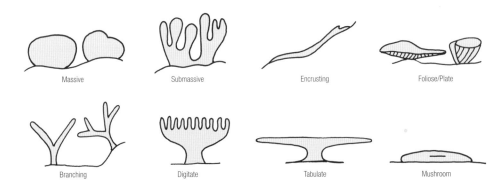

Massive   Submassive   Encrusting   Foliose/Plate

Branching   Digitate   Tabulate   Mushroom

Agariciidae

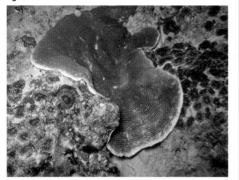

Pachyseris speciosa
Colonies vary from brown to grey, usually with a pale border and tend to be foliose or encrusting. Parallel ridges run along the coral's surface. FO/EN

Pavona explanulata
Found in a variety of colours including brown, pink, purple, green and yellow. Colonies are encrusting or plate-like and occasionally submassive. A common species in Seychelles. FO/EN/SM

Pavona clavus
Tends to be pale in colour, often beige or grey. Colonies are club-shaped and can cover large areas of the reef. Coral's surface is pitted with numerous small, fine, star-shaped corallites. SM

Acroporidae

Acropora spp.
The genus Acropora is a group of fast-growing, reef-building corals common on reefs throughout Seychelles. They are categorized by having an axial corallite and come in a variety of colours and life-forms, ranging from small encrusting colonies to huge table corals. There are numerous species that have a similar appearance, making them difficult to identify. EN/BR/D/TA

Astreopora myriophthalma
Colonies can be yellow, cream, brown or blue and are encrusting or boulder-shaped, with an even, granulated surface covered in small conical corallites. EN/MA

Euphyllidae

Physogyra lichtensteini
Colonies are usually grey or beige. Polyp tentacles are extended at night, and during the day the colony is covered in translucent, bubble-shaped vesicles. A common species on Seychelles reefs. MA/EN

Turbinaria reniformis
Colonies have corallites only on one side and form plate-like tiers, usually horizontally. The surface of the coral is smooth with widely spaced, conical corallites. FO/EN

Dendrophylliidae

Tubastrea aurea
Found in orange, yellow, pink and red colourations. Lacks zooxanthellae and is commonly found under ledges and in caves. Cup-shaped corallites house large polyps with delicate tentacles, which are extended at night. SM

Faviidae

Diploastrea heliopora
Usually grey, green or brown. Colonies are dome-shaped and can be up to 2 m (6½ ft) high. They have distinctive cone- or doughnut-shaped corallites with small openings and thick walls. MA/EN

Tubastrea micrantha
Dark green or black with numerous branches and large tube-like polyps. This species lacks zooxanthellae and is usually found below 15 m (50 ft) depth. BR

Echinopora hirsutissima
Colonies are yellow, green, brown or purple. They are encrusting with numerous prominent corallites covering the surface. EN

Echinopora lamellosa
Lavender, pale to dark brown or green. Thin plate-like colonies are arranged in whorls with what look like water droplets on their surface. Can reach up to 5 m (16 ft) in diameter. FO

Goniastrea pectinata
Colonies tend to be pink or brown and are encrusting or submassive. Corallite walls are thick and meandering. Prefers shallow water reef environments. EN/SM

Favia spp.
A genus of hard corals containing several similar species. Colonies are found in a variety of colours and commonly at granitic sites in Seychelles. Species in this genus are characterized by each corallite having its own walls. EN/MA

Montrastrea serageldini
Grey, brown, pink or orange but always with lighter oral discs. Colonies are massive with numerous uniform, circular corallites that have the appearance of upturned bottle-tops. This species does not grow beyond 1 m (3 ft) in diameter. MA

Favites spp.
Favites is a genus comprised of several similar looking species. Corals in this genus differ from *Favia* spp. in that the corallites share walls. Corallites can vary widely in size between species in this genus. EN/MA

Platygyra acuta
Colony walls are brown and thin with deep, green valleys that meander. Corals are boulder shaped and can be common in shallow reef environments. MA

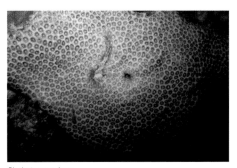

Plesiastrea versipora
Found in a variety of colours, including beige, yellow, brown and green. Colonies tend to be small and flat, and prefer overhangs and caves. Polyp tentacles are sometimes extended during the day giving an appearance of eyelashes. EN

Herpolitha limax
Grey to brown, elongate free-living colonies. Sometimes forked to produce Y, T or X shapes. Polyp tentacles are retracted during the day. MU

Fungiidae

Fungia spp.
This genus contains several similar species, most of which are free-living and do not attach to the substrate. They are usually round or oval with a central slit-shaped mouth, and can be brown, pink, blue or grey in colour. MU

Polyphyllia talpina
Grey, green or brown with white tips to the tentacles. The numerous, long tentacles are extended during the day. These corals are not attached to the substrate but are free living. MU

Mussidae

Halomitra pileus
Brown with purple or pink margins. Colonies are dome shaped and free living. An uncommon species around the inner islands, it is usually found in areas not subject to wave action. MU

Acanthastrea brevis
Yellow, brown or occasionally green. An encrusting species forming small colonies with thick walls, closed corallites and spiky projections on the corallite walls. More commonly found on granitic sites. EN

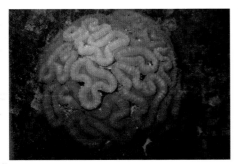

Lobophyllia hemprichii
Corallite walls are thick and fleshy with a smooth or rough mantle. Colonies vary in colour and grow in a hemispherical shape, and can be several metres across. SM

Pectiniidae

Echinophyllia aspera
Brown or green, colonies are thin and plate-like with prominent raised corallites. Usually found in areas of low wave action. FO

Symphyllia radians
Colonies can be red, green or grey, often with contrasting coloured valleys and walls. Young corals tend to be encrusting, becoming massive as they grow. Walls are thick and fleshy with a groove running down the centre. Found on carbonate reefs. EN/MA

Mycedium elephantotus
Brown, grey, green or pink with green, white or red oral discs. Large nose-shaped corallites face the coral perimeter. Tentacles are extended at night. Found in areas protected from wave action. FO/EN

Oculinidae

Galaxea fascicularis
Can be red, grey or brown, but commonly green with contrasting tentacles. Colonies are encrusting or massive and can be extremely common in some areas. Tentacles are usually extended during the day. EN/MA

Pocilloporidae

Pocillopora damicornis
Pink, green or brown. Colonies are branching and compact, often found in shallow water and in areas of high wave action. Small black verrucae cover the coral's surface. The smallest of the Pocillopora species, it is a common coral in Seychelles. BR

Pocillopora eydouxi
Brown, purple or green. Colonies are often large with upright, flattened branches that are widely spaced and home to Rust-spotted Guard Crabs. The coral's surface is also covered in small black verrucae. A common coral around the inner islands. BR

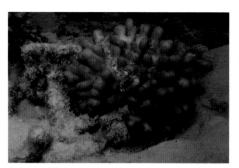

Stylophora pistillata
Green, purple, pink or cream. Colonies have blunt-ended branches, which tend to be thicker in areas of high wave action and can have the appearance of teddy bear's legs. BR

Poritidae

Goniopora lobata
Brown to red or green, colonies form domes or columns. Polyps are long and have 24 tentacles on each stalk, they are nearly always extended unless wafted vigorously. A very common species on the reefs of the inner islands. Can cause an irritation to the skin if touched. MA/SM

Porites spp.
Often cream or brown but sometimes purple. Colonies are large and boulder shaped with a smooth surface. Common in shallow water where they form micro-atolls. A slow-growing coral species. Two similar-looking species *P. lobata* and *P. lutea* are found in Seychelles. EN/MA

Siderastreidae

Psammocora digitata
Grey, purple or brown colonies are submassive forming tall columns. Shallow corallites are small and numerous, with polyps usually extended giving the coral a fuzzy appearance. SM

Psammocora obtusangula
Beige, yellow or grey. Small branching colonies can be loosely attached to the substrate. Irregular branching coral with densely packed corallites. Often found in shallow reef environments. BR

Phylum Platyhelminthes and Annelida

Flatworms
Phylum Platyhelminthes
Order Polycladida

With their flattened, elongate bodies, and bright colours, flatworms can be confused with nudibranchs. They are, however, worms and not molluscs and belong to a different Phylum. Flatworms range in size from less than 1 cm to over 10 cm (⅜ to 4 in). They spend the majority of their time hidden in the reef but are sometimes seen crawling across the substrate. Many species are also capable of swimming, which they do through an undulating motion.

Pseudocerotidae

Fine-lined Flatworm   *Pseudoceros monostichos*
Size to 4 cm (1½ in)
White to cream body with black dorsal stripe bordered by a brown band either side. Marginal band blue to purple.

Brilliant Flatworm   *Pseudoceros scintillatus*
Size to 3 cm (1¼ in)
Black body with numerous white to yellow spots and orange marginal band. Often found in seagrass or rubble in shallow water.

Suzanne's Flatworm   *Pseudoceros susanae*
Size to 3 cm (1¼ in)
Vivid marginal band colouration ranging from blue to violet, with a central white stripe bordered by orange bands.

Feather duster worms and tube worms
Phylum Annelida
Class Polychaeta
Feather duster and tube worms do not appear to be worms at all, as their bodies are hidden inside long tube-like structures. Only the feathery gill appendages are seen, which are used to capture plankton from the water. These worms are very sensitive to disturbance and instantly retract into their tubes when closely approached.

Sabellidae

Indian Feather Duster Worm   *Sabellastarte spectabilis*
Size to 10 cm (4 in)
Branched tentacles are striped with alternating light and dark bands. Disappears into tube when disturbed.

Serpulidae

Christmas Tree Worm   *Spirobranchus* sp.
Size to 3 cm (1¼ in)
Found in a variety of colours. Has pair of tapering, spiral gills extending from a calcareous tube buried within the substrate.

Terebellidae

Spaghetti Worm   N/A
Size to 100 cm (40 in)
Long translucent white tentacles, sometimes with markings. Segmented body usually hidden within the reef. Tentacles will retract if touched.

Phylum Arthropoda

Shrimps, lobsters and crabs Order Decapoda and Stomatapoda
Species in this Order are distinguished by having five pairs of legs, and most have evolved the first pair of legs into claws for feeding and defence. Shrimps can be identified by their long hair-like antennae and laterally compressed bodies. Many shrimps are symbiotic with species of anemone, sea cucumber or urchin. Lobsters are nocturnal and live on the bottom of the reef. They have long, well developed antennae and strong legs for walking, although they can swim in a backward motion when threatened. There is a huge variety of crabs in the marine environment. Most have a large, round, flattened carapace and do not have noticeable antennae.

Odontodactylidae

Peacock Mantis Shrimp   *Odontodactylus scyllarus*
Size to 18 cm (7 in)
Male is dark green and female orange/yellow. They have blue eye stalks and complex compound eyes. These shrimps are capable of punching with speed equivalent to a .22 calibre bullet. Often found hunting away from their burrows.

Palaemonidae

Peacock-tail Anemone   *Periclimenes brevicarpalis*
Size to 4 cm (1½ in)
Translucent body with white blotches and purple appendages. Five orange spots with black margin on the tail. Commensal with a number of species of anemone.

Hippolytidae

White-banded Cleaner Shrimp   *Lysmata amboinensis*
Size to 6 cm (2½ in)
Orange/yellow body with red dorsal surface bisected by a white stripe. Often observed removing parasites from fishes.

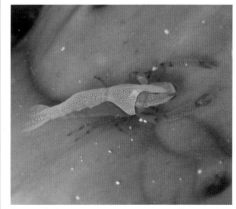

Emperor Shrimp   *Zenopontonia rex*
Size to 2 cm (¾ in)
Frequently red with white blotches on the dorsal area, though colour variants do exist. Found in association with a number of sea cucumber species.

Rhynchocinetidae

Hingebeak Shrimp   *Rhynchocinetes durbanensis*
Size to 4 cm (1½ in)
Red body and legs with white lines and dots. Distinctive humpback body shape. Often found in large aggregations in crevices and under ledges.

Stenopodidae

Banded Coral Shrimp   *Stenopus hispidus*
Size to 5 cm (2 in)
White body with red/brown bands. Elongated claw arms and antennae. Found in crevices on the reef where they remove parasites from fish. Circumtropical.

Palinuridae

Painted Lobster   *Panulirus versicolor*
Size to 40 cm (16 in)
Black carapace with yellow stripes and green abdomen. White lines on the carapace and on the edges of abdomen segments. Nocturnal. Usually found hiding under coral outcrops and ledges during the day.

Pronghorn Spiny Lobster   *Panulirus longipes*
Size to 30 cm (12 in)
Yellowish/green to reddish brown carapace. Abdomen covered in numerous white spots, with blue at base of antennae. Found under ledges and corals in shallow water.

Porcellanidae

Porcelain Crab   *Neopetrolisthes maculatus*
Size to 3 cm (1¼ in)
White with fine red spots. Often observed with raised feeding appendages sieving microscopic plankton from the current. Commensal with anemones.

Trapeziidae

Rust-spotted Guard Crab   *Trapezia rufopunctata*
Size to 5 cm (2 in)
Cream body with numerous red spots. In Seychelles it is found in association with *Pocillopora eydouxi* where it hides at the base of the coral branches.

Phylum Mollusca

Found on land, in freshwater and within the marine environment, approximately 85,000 species of molluscs have been classified to date and they account for almost a quarter of all marine organisms. The word 'Mollusca' comes from the Latin meaning 'soft bodied', and perfectly describes the members of this Phylum. While many molluscs have a calcium carbonate shell, which is secreted from the mantle, this is not always present and there is a huge amount of anatomical diversity within the Phylum.

Snails Class Gastropoda
Gastropods are the most common group of molluscs, containing over 35,000 species worldwide. Many gastropods have a single shell, which they are able to withdraw into when threatened. However, in some families the shell is reduced in size or completely absent. Several gastropod species have a well-developed head that contains sensory organs.

Cypraeidae

Tiger Cowrie   *Cypraea tigris*
Size to 5 cm (6 in)
Shell is white with numerous black spots with red to brown outlines. The mantle is translucent with fine lines and is covered in long white-tipped filaments. A common cowrie in shallow waters.

Strombidae

Giant Spider Conch   *Lambis* sp.
Size to 40 cm (16 in)
Found on rubble or sandy substrate. Large shell with finger-like projections emanating from the edge of the shell's aperture.

Ovulidae

Egg Cowrie   *Ovula ovum*
Size to 10 cm (4 in)
A large white shell with a black mantle covered in small white spots. Feeds on leather corals.

Muricidae

Ramose Murex   *Chicoreus ramosus*
Size to 25 cm (10 in)
A large shell with numerous long protrusions. Often covered in calcareous algae and well camouflaged against substrate.

Sap-sucking slugs and nudibranchs   Subclass Opisthobranchia

Opisthobranchs are also known as sea slugs and include a number of different Orders including sea hares, sap-sucking slugs and nudibranchs. The species in this subclass are characterized by the absence of a shell, although a handful of species do retain a poorly developed internal or external shell. The majority of sea slugs possess a pair of sensory organs known as rhinophores, which they use for smell and taste, while other species also have oral tentacles.

Nudibranchs, which are by far the most common Order of sea slugs, are often brightly coloured and many species have a set of gills, known as a branchial plume, located on their back. Usually only a few centimetres long, they are found in a variety of habitats including sandy substrates, seagrass beds and on coral reefs. Many species are diurnal though some, like the giant Spanish Dancer, are likely to be seen at night when they are more active.

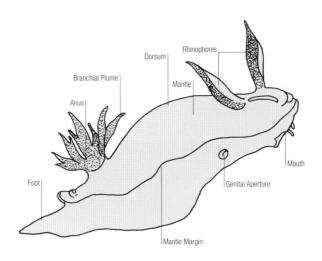

Parts of a generalized nudibranch species.

Caliphyllidae

Black and Gold Cycerce   *Cycerce nigricans*
Size to 4 cm (1½ in)
Numerous black cerata with vivid orange spots and margins. Able to shed their cerata to avoid predation.

Chromodorididae

White-spotted Goniobranchus   *Goniobranchus albopunctatus*
Size to 5 cm (2 in)
Two colour forms present: one yellow and one red, both with pale speckling. Both have a yellow and blue marginal band.

Twin Goniobranchus *Goniobranchus geminus*
Size to 7 cm (2¾ in)
Bright yellow rhinophores and dorsum with large dark spots ringed in white. Mantle with alternating yellow, white and blue marginal band. Often observed raising its mantle skirt.

Gleniei's Goniobranchus *Goniobranchus gleniei*
Size to 5 cm (2 in)
Orange rhinophores and dorsum with black markings. Creamy mantle edge and branchial plume. Raises the front of the mantle skirt to reveal a purple underside.

Girdled Glossodoris *Glossodoris cincta*
Size to 10 cm (4 in)
Pink to reddish brown body with small white spots. Marginal band is blue and green, and is highly ruffled.

Beautiful Hypselodoris *Hypselodoris pulchella*
Size to 12 cm (4¾ in)
White to cream body covered in yellow/orange spots. Purple edge to mantle and foot. Often displays tailing behaviour.

Discodoridae

Tessellated Halgerda   *Halgerda tessellata*
Size to 5 cm (2 in)
A network of black-margined, orange ridges with white and black spots in between. Pale rhinophores with black edge.

Facelinidae

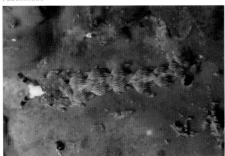

Serpent Pteraeolidia   *Pteraeolidia ianthina*
Size to 10 cm (4 in)
Highly variable in colour, ranging from brown to blue and purple. Elongated body with numerous groups of cerata. Purple bands on rhinophores and oral tentacles. This species stores symbiotic zooxanthellae in its cerata.

Hexabranchidae

Spanish Dancer   *Hexabranchus sanguineus*
Size to 60 cm (24 in)
Variable in colour ranging from red to orange and often with bands or mottling. Six separate gill branches. Swim by flapping their mantle. Nocturnal although occasionally found during the day.

Phyllidiidae

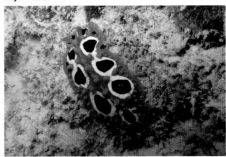

Ocellate Phyllidia   *Phyllidia ocellata*
Size to 5 cm (2 in)
Variable colouration and pattern. Orange, black and white in colouration. Rhinophores are always orange/yellow.

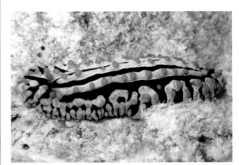

Swollen Phyllidia   *Phyllidia varicosa*
Size to 12 cm (4¾ in)
Blue longitudinal ridges down body with yellow warty spots and yellow rhinophores. Black valleys between the ridges. A very common species.

Polyceridae

Lined Nembrotha   *Nembrotha lineolata*
Size to 6 cm (2½ in)
Tan undercolour with brown lines running the length of the body. Blue to purple rings around the base of rhinophores and branchial plume. Commonly seen at L'ilot dive site.

Oysters and clams Class Bivalvia

Bivalves are a diverse group of molluscs with over 9,000 species identified worldwide. They include oysters, clams, scallops, mussels and a variety of other species. The name 'bivalve' describes the paired shell of the animal, which is held together by a flexible hinge and can be closed tightly by its strong abductor muscles. The majority of bivalves house a large gill within their mantle cavity. This is used to extract oxygen from the water and sieve passing food from the current.

Gryphaeidae

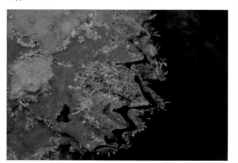

Honeycomb Oyster *Hyotissa hyotis*
Size to 25 cm (10 in)
The shell is commonly encrusted with sponge and other organisms. The shell opening has a pronounced zigzag pattern. Attached to granite rocks and reef walls, it quickly closes if disturbed.

Tridacnidae

Fluted Giant Clam *Tridacna squamosa*
Size to 40 cm (16 in)
Mantle colouration is highly variable ranging from blue to green to purple. The shell has rows of ridged protrusions. Can grow to 40 cm (16 in), though rarely reaches that size within the inner islands.

Octopus and squid Class Cephalopoda

Cephalopods are the most highly evolved of all the invertebrates, with a complex nervous system and excellent vision. This Class includes octopus, squid, cuttlefish and nautilus. All cephalopods are carnivorous, equipped with long powerful arms and a beak-like mouth to capture and crush their prey. They move by jet propulsion, propelling water through a siphon in their mantle.

Cephalopods are perhaps most famous for their capacity to change colour. Numerous pigment-filled cells, known as chromatophores, allow for a sudden change in colour, enabling the animal to blend in with the substrate and avoid detection, or to communicate with other members of the same species.

While nautilus usually inhabit deep water and cuttlefish are not found around the Seychelles inner islands, both octopus and squid are common sightings.

Octopodidae

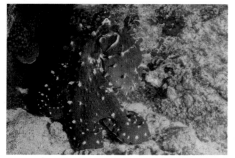

Common Octopus *Octopus cyanea*
Size to 80 cm (32 in)
Wide variety of colour patterns. They have the ability to change colour and skin texture. Usually inhabit rock and rubble reef. Their holes are identifiable by the discarded crustacean and mollusc shells around the entrance.

Loliginidae

Bigfin Reef Squid *Sepioteuthis lessoniana*
Size to 35 cm (14 in)
Highly variable colour with the ability to change pattern and colour. Usually in small groups though large localized aggregations form to mate and lay white egg cases at certain times of the year.

Phylum Echinodermata

Sea stars, brittle stars, sea urchins and sea cucumbers are classed as echinoderms and in total number approximately 7,000 species around the world. They possess a unique vascular system made up of a network of fluid-filled cavities. Echinoderms are benthic organisms and are found in a variety of habitats, including seagrass beds, sandy substrates and on coral reefs. Some families, such as the sea cucumbers, are commercially valuable, which has led to the development of a carefully managed fishery in Seychelles.

Sea stars Class Asteroidea
Sea stars are found in a variety of colours and sizes. Many species have five arms, although some can have more, but all species remain unattached from the substrate. The arms radiate from a central disc and in most species they narrow to a point. The mouth is located centrally on the underside of the sea star and rows of suction discs extend from the mouth along the length of each arm. Sea stars have the remarkable ability to regenerate broken or damaged arms.

Acanthasteridae

Crown-of-thorns Starfish   *Acanthaster planci*
Size to 40 cm (16 in)
Variable colouration from red to yellow to purple. Numerous spine-covered arms contain a toxin. A voracious corallivore, population explosions have occurred around the inner islands, possibly due to excess nutrient loading.

Ophidiasteridae

Blue Sea Star *Linckia laevigata*
Size to 30 cm (12 in)
Can vary in colour though specimens within the inner islands are more frequently blue. The yellow and blue forms are shown. A common sea star.

Ophidiasteridae

Oreasteridae

Noduled Sea Star *Fromia nodosa*
Size to 10 cm (4 in)
Bright red body with cream-coloured layers forming a chain-like pattern.

Cushion Star *Culcita novaeguineae*
Size to 25 cm (10 in)
A large inflated sea star with a pentagonal shape. Variable colouration including red, purple, green and brown. Feeds on *Acropora* spp. and *Pocillopora* spp.

Ophidiasteridae

Oreasteridae

Brown Mesh Sea Star *Nardoa galatheae*
Size to 20 cm (8 in)
Dark brown sea star with red/orange spot pattern in rows down tapered, cylindrical arms.

Granular Sea Star *Choriaster granulatus*
Size to 25 cm (10 in)
Red, orange or tan with short thick arms. Arm tips are either lighter or darker than the body of the sea star.

115

Urchins *Class Echinoidea*
The class Echinoidea, which includes sea urchins, is characterized by species that have external skeletons with numerous spines. There are many types of sea urchin, all of which have spherical bodies covered in protective spines. These spines can differ in length and shape, varying from short and blunt to extremely sharp and fragile. As with sea stars, the mouth is located centrally on the underside of the animal. Many species of sea urchin spend the day hidden out of view, preferring to come out at night to feed.

Echinometridae

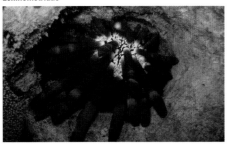

Slate Pencil Urchin *Heterocentrotus mammillatus*
Size to 8 cm (3¼ in)
Inhabits crevices in shallow carbonate reefs. Red to brown body with large, pencil-sized blunt spines, often with light or dark bands.

Diadematidae

Shortspined Sea Urchin *Echinothrix diadema*
Size to 20 cm (8 in)
Black or dark blue with numerous spines. Active at night, preferring to spend the day hiding in crevices.

Diadematidae

Longspined Sea Urchin *Diadema setosum*
Size to 30 cm (12 in)
Black with numerous spines that are longer than the diameter of its body. Has prominent red ring around anus opening on top of the body, and five white spots on body.

Echinometridae

Mathae's Urchin *Echinometra mathaei*
Size to 5 cm (2 in)
Oval body, burgundy or purple in colour. Sharp-pointed spines with a white ring around the base. Lodges in the reef where it bores into the limestone structure.

Toxopneustidae

Flower Urchin *Toxopneustes pileolus*
Size to 5 cm (6 in)
Pale pink body with short spines and flower-like tubular feet. Often covered with debris and rubble, they inhabit very shallow water including sand and seagrass beds. Can inflict a painful sting.

Toxopneustidae

Cake Urchin *Tripneustes gratilla*
Size to 10 cm (4 in)
Spherical dark brown to purple body covered with fine white to reddish spines, separated by 10 spineless bands giving the appearance of a sliced cake. Often covered with debris.

Sea cucumbers Class Holothurians

Sea cucumbers tend to have elongated bodies with a mouth and an anus at opposite ends. Some species possess a set of feeding tentacles around the mouth, while others have tube-like feet called podia that they use to feed. The colour of sea cucumbers is highly variable with many species well camouflaged to blend in with their surroundings. Some sea cucumbers can be found moving slowly across the substrate whilst others spend much of their time buried beneath the sand.

Holothuriidae

Yellow Surffish *Actinopyga mauritania*
Size to 25 cm (10 in)
Smooth brown to green surface with white patches, has appearance of cracked mud. Usually found in shallow water between 1 – 3 m (3 – 10 ft) depth.

Holothuriidae

Tigerfish *Bohadschia atra*
Size to 40 cm (16 in)
Dark brown to black with numerous target-like red spots. Found in seagrass beds and shallow reef areas.

Holothuriidae

Flowerfish *Pearsonothuria graeffei*
Size to 40 cm (16 in)
Cream to brown with mottled patches. Has a mouth on the underside of the body with black, flower-shaped, feeding tentacles. Juveniles mimic a toxic nudibranch. One of the most common sea cucumbers in Seychelles.

Holothuriidae

Elephant Trunk *Holothuria fuscopunctata*
Size to 70 cm (28 in)
Cream to grey with light ventral surface and darker dorsal area with numerous spots. Ridges run across the body giving a characteristic wrinkled appearance.

Stichopodidae

Greenfish *Stichopus chloronotus*
Size to 35 cm (14 in)
Cylindrical body, dark green in colour with elongate papillae running the length of the body in rows. Usually inhabits rocky and rubble areas.

Stichopodidae

Prickly Redfish *Thelenota ananas*
Size to 70 cm (28 in)
Red to brown with spine-like papillae covering the body. Inhabits sand and rubble often found living in association with Emperor Shrimp (*Zenopontonia rex*).

Phylum Chordata

Fish Class Osteichthyes
It is not easy to provide a definition of what a fish is, but a brief explanation would be 'an aquatic vertebrate, with gills, scales and fins'. However, confusingly some of these characteristics are shared with other animal groups and not all fish possess all of the above features. The Class Osteichthyes includes all fish that have a backbone.

Marine fishes come in an endless variety of forms, and range in size from only a couple of centimetres long to over 3 m (1 in – 6 ft), as in the case of the Ocean Sunfish. The diversity of body shape is also impressive and ranges from elongated trumpetfish, to flatfish and snake-like moray eels.

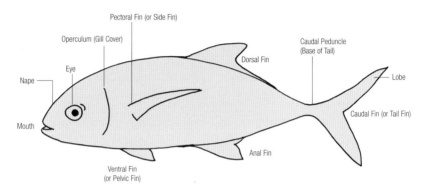

Parts of a generalized fish species.

The shape of a fish's body can convey information about its lifestyle. A torpedo-shaped body with pointed fins indicates a pelagic fish built for speed, such as a tuna. A grouper, on the other hand, has large, rounded fins, which reveals a lifestyle closely associated to the reef, where slower movements are required.

Differences in body shape can even be used to distinguish between families. An example of this is the butterflyfish and angelfish, which are both brightly coloured fish families frequently encountered on Seychelles reefs. While they may appear similar at first glance, angelfish have convex napes, while butterflyfish have concave napes. Add to this the fact that angelfish all possess a spine on their gill cover, and it is possible to easily distinguish between the two families.

In addition to body shape, body markings can assist with the identification of fish species. The diagram below gives examples of the different types of markings as well as the terms used in the fish identification section.

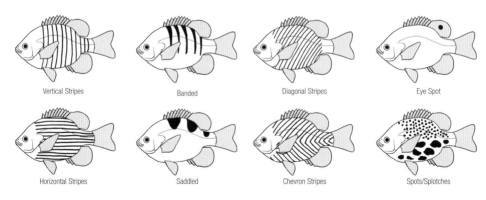

Fish markings.

Damselfish, anemonefish and chromis (Pomacentridae)

Scissortail Sergeant *Abudefduf sexfasciatus*
Size to 17 cm (6¾ in)
White body with five black bars and black scissor-like borders to the tail. Feeds on zooplankton and found to a depth of 15 m (50 ft). Very common and forms large aggregations in the water column.

Two-tone Damsel *Chromis dimidiata*
Size to 7 cm (2¾ in)
Black head and forebody with white rear body and tail. Solitary or small groups close to the substrate.

Skunk Anemonefish *Amphiprion akallopisos*
Size to 10 cm (4 in)
Pink to orange with distinctive white dorsal stripe running from head to tail. Found in association with the anemone *Stichodactyla mertensii* and will occasionally share an anemone with *Amphiprion fuscocaudatus*.

Ternate Chromis *Chromis ternatensis*
Size to 10 cm (4 in)
Silver body with yellow hue on the back. Black borders to the tail. Found in aggregations near *Acropora* spp.

Seychelles Anemonefish *Amphiprion fuscocaudatus*
Size to 14 cm (5½ in)
Black to orange body with two prominent white bars. Caudal peduncle and tail margins white. Endemic to Seychelles where it associates with the anemone *Stichodactyla mertensii*. Can be territorial.

Blue-green Chromis *Chromis viridis*
Size to 9 cm (3½ in)
Blue to green iridescent body and fins. Forms large schools above the reef, sheltering in branching corals when threatened. An extremely abundant chromis in Seychelles.

Humbug Dascyllus *Dascyllus aruanus*
Size to 8 cm (3¼ in)
White with three black bars and a black ventral fin. A shallow water species often found on reef flats where it hides among the branches of *Acropora* spp. and *Pocillopora* spp. corals.

Dick's Damsel *Plectroglyphidodon dickii*
Size to 11 cm (4¼ in)
Gold body and orange tail with V-shaped clear margin. Black bar towards rear of body. Associated with *Pocillopora* spp. and *Acropora* spp. corals.

Indian Dascyllus *Dascyllus carneus*
Size to 8 cm (3¼ in)
Tan body with black bar behind the head and a second at the base of the tail. Blue spots on the face, dorsal fin rays and edges of tail. Seeks shelter in branching corals. Very common.

Caerulean Damsel *Pomacentrus caeruleus*
Size to 8 cm (3¼ in)
Neon blue body with yellow underside and yellow pelvic, anal and caudal fins. Forms loose aggregations above rubble and coral.

Three-spot Dascyllus *Dascyllus trimaculatus*
Size to 14 cm (5½ in)
Dark grey sometimes with yellow tinge to the head. Juveniles black with large white spot on the forehead and on each side of the back. Sometimes associated with anemones, which they share with species of anemonefish.

Sulphur Damsel *Pomacentrus sulfureus*
Size to 11 cm (4¼ in)
Yellow body and fins with blue to purple speckling on the face and a black spot at the base of the pectoral fin. A common territorial species in areas of shallow reef.

Butterflyfish (Chaetodontidae)

Threadfin Butterflyfish *Chaetodon auriga*
Size to 23 cm (9 in)
Chevron markings on a white body give way to a yellow rear and tail. Black spot on dorsal fin with thread-like filament. Common on carbonate reefs where it is solitary or forms small groups.

Racoon Butterflyfish *Chaetodon lunula*
Size to 20 cm (8 in)
Yellow body with black eye mask and white area behind. Black spot on the caudal peduncle. Solitary, pairs or small groups.

Spotted Butterflyfish *Chaetodon guttatissimus*
Size to 12 cm (4¾ in)
Silver to beige with light speckling on the body. The dorsal fin exhibits a yellow margin and there is a black band on the tail fin. Solitary or in pairs.

Black-backed Butterflyfish *Chaetodon melannotus*
Size to 5 cm (6 in)
White body with yellow margins and black diagonal lines. Black shading to the upper rear half of the body. Solitary or in pairs, feeds on the polyps of soft and hard corals.

Klein's Butterflyfish *Chaetodon kleinii*
Size to 14 cm (5½ in)
Orange/brown body, white head with black bar through eye. Usually in pairs but also solitary and in aggregations. Typically found below 10 m (33 ft).

Meyer's Butterflyfish *Chaetodon meyeri*
Size to 20 cm (8 in)
White body with yellow rim and broad, curved, black bands. Usually found in pairs, this butterflyfish feeds exclusively on coral polyps.

Chevroned Butterflyfish *Chaetodon trifascialis*
Size to 18 cm (7 in)
Rectangular white body with black chevron markings and a black tail with yellow margin. Solitary or in pairs, usually associated with tabular Acropora corals.

Yellowheaded Butterflyfish *Chaetodon xanthocephalus*
Size to 20 cm (8 in)
Yellow/orange head with grey body and yellow/orange dorsal and anal fins. A territorial species which is often solitary or in pairs.

Indian Redfin Butterflyfish *Chaetodon trifasciatus*
Size to 5 cm (6 in)
Pale body with pinstripe pattern and red anal fin. Usually in pairs, occasionally small groups. Feeds exclusively on coral polyps. By far the most common butterflyfish species within the inner islands.

Longnosed Butterflyfish *Forcipiger flavissimus*
Size to 22 cm (8¾ in)
Yellow body with black upper part to the head and silver below. Black spot on the anal fin. Distinctive elongated snout. Solitary or in pairs. An uncommon species within the inner granitic islands.

Zanzibar Butterflyfish *Chaetodon zanzibariensis*
Size to 12 cm (4¾ in)
Yellow body with black bar through the eye and black spot on middle of the back. Common on Seychelles reefs where they are solitary, in pairs or small groups. Feeds on a variety of corals.

Longfin Bannerfish *Heniochus acuminatus*
Size to 25 cm (10 in)
White body with two broad black bands and elongated dorsal fin filament. Feeds on zooplankton and invertebrates. Solitary, in pairs or small aggregations.

Angelfish (Pomacanthidae)

Three-spot Angelfish *Apolemichthys trimaculatus*
Size to 25 cm (10 in)
Yellow body with bright blue lips and black spot on the nape. Black margin on the anal fin. A common angelfish on Seychelles reefs. Solitary or in pairs.

Emperor Angelfish (juvenile) *Pomacanthus imperator*
Size to 8 cm (3¼ in)
Blue-black with vivid white concentric rings. Fades into adult colouration as they grow. Solitary, and hides in crevices.

African Pygmy Angelfish *Centropyge acanthops*
Size to 7 cm (2¾ in)
Bright orange head and dorsal fin, blue body and yellow translucent tail. Forms small groups in areas of branching coral and rubble. Difficult to approach.

Emperor Angelfish *Pomacanthus imperator*
Size to 40 cm (16 in)
Black eye mask with electric blue edge. Alternating blue and yellow stripes and yellow tail. Solitary or in pairs. Makes a loud drumming sound when alarmed.

Many-spined Angelfish *Centropyge multispinis*
Size to 9 cm (3½ in)
Brown body with thin dark bars and a large ear spot. Ventral fins bright blue. A common species found over coral rubble.

Regal Angelfish *Pygoplites diacanthus*
Size to 25 cm (10 in)
Yellow/orange with blue/white bars with dark margins. Solitary or in pairs. The least common of the large angelfish species within the inner islands.

Semicircle Angelfish (juvenile) *Pomacanthus semicirculatus*
Size to 16 cm (6¼ in)
Blue-black body similar to juvenile *P. imperator*, though white bands form semicircles instead. Found in shallow water hiding amongst coral and rubble.

Semicircle Angelfish *Pomacanthus semicirculatus*
Size to 38 cm (15 in)
Green to gold body with blue spots and yellow lips. Bright blue margin to operculum and cheek spine. A common angelfish species.

Surgeonfish, Tangs and Unicornfish (Acanthuridae)

Powderblue Surgeonfish *Acanthurus leucosternon*
Size to 23 cm (9 in)
Black head with a powder blue body and yellow dorsal fin. Common on granitic reefs, less so on carbonate reefs. Algal grazer found between 0.5 – 25 m (1 – 80 ft).

Yellow Surgeonfish *Acanthurus xanthopterus*
Size to 60 cm (24 in)
Grey to purple with yellow eye mask. Yellow edge to pectoral, dorsal and pelvic fins.

Striped Surgeonfish *Acanthurus lineatus*
Size to 38 cm (15 in)
Alternating gold and blue stripes with black margins. A common surgeonfish on granitic reefs where it is found shallower than 10 m (33 ft) . Very territorial.

Convict Surgeonfish *Acanthurus triostegus*
Size to 26 cm (10¼ in)
White body with widely spaced thin black bars. Found on carbonate reefs in shallow water, usually less than 5 m (16 ft). Feeds on algae, often forming large schools.

Palette Surgeonfish   *Paracanthurus hepatus*
Size to 30 cm (12 in)
Bright blue body with black markings and yellow tail with black borders. Found on granitic reefs where juveniles hide within branching corals. Feeds on zooplankton.

Indian Goldring Bristletooth   *Ctenochaetus truncatus*
Size to 18 cm (7 in)
Brown body with pale spots on the head. Distinctive yellow ring around the eye and yellow edge to the pectoral fins.

Indian Sailfin Tang   *Zebrasoma desjardinii*
Size to 40 cm (16 in)
Alternating light and dark bars with elongated dorsal and anal fins. Juveniles have similar appearance but yellow body with dark bars. Solitary or in small groups.

Orangespine Unicornfish   *Naso elegans*
Size to 45 cm (18 in)
A large unicornfish, grey to black in colour with a yellow nape and orange tail spines. Also has trailing tail fin. Solitary or forms small groups, feeds on macro algae.

Moorish Idol (Zanclidae)

Moorish Idol   *Zanclus cornutus*
Size to 16 cm (6¼ in)
Alternating black and yellow/white bars. Yellow saddle on the snout and a filamentous dorsal fin. Solitary, pairs or small groups.

Twospot Bristletooth   *Ctenochaetus binotatus*
Size to 22 cm (8¾ in)
Orange to brown body with distinctive blue ring around the eye and black spot at the base of the dorsal and anal fin. Feeds on detritus and algae.

125

Rabbitfish (Siganidae)

Coral Rabbitfish   *Siganus corallinus*
Size to 30 cm (12 in)
Yellow body with small blue spots. Usually in pairs, though sometimes forms large aggregations. Feeds on macro algae and sponges.

Honeycomb Rabbitfish   *Siganus stellatus*
Size to 35 cm (14 in)
Covered in dark, polygon-shaped spots giving a honeycomb appearance. Rear dorsal and forked tail fin has a white edge. Usually in pairs.

Forktail Rabbitfish   *Siganus argenteus*
Size to 33 cm (13 in)
Yellow nape and pectoral fin, with yellow spots across body. Colour variable from blue to bluish/grey and quickly changes to a mottled pattern when at rest. Forms large schools and often inhabits seagrass beds where they feed on macro algae.

Wrasse (Labridae)

Tripletail Wrasse   *Cheilinus trilobatus*
Size to 45 cm (18 in)
Green undercolour with ornate pink pattern covering the head. Adults have pair of white bars on the tail and a third lobe in the middle of tail fin. Solitary and usually wary of divers.

Humphead Wrasse   *Cheilinus undulatus*
Size to 220 cm (87 in)
Green body with dark streaks and network of patterns on the head. Adults with prominent hump on the forehead. Solitary or occasionally in pairs. One of the largest reef fish, globally numbers are declining due to overfishing.

Sixbar Wrasse   *Thalassoma hardwicke*
Size to 20 cm (8 in)
Light green body colour with six black bars, pink markings radiating from the eye. Often encountered on shallow reefs where it feeds on crustaceans and small fishes.

Checkerboard Wrasse *Halichoeres hortulanus*
Size to 27 cm (10½ in)
Pink/orange bands on the head with yellow fins. Checkerboard appearance on body with blue bars on each scale. Feeds on small invertebrates buried in the sand.

Rockmover Wrasse *Novaculichthys taeniourus*
Size to 27 cm (10½ in)
Grey to green head with lines radiating from the eye. Dark body with white tail band. A solitary species, commonly observed turning over small rocks in search of prey.

Blackedge Thicklip Wrasse *Hemigymnus melapterus*
Size to 50 cm (20 in)
Grey head and front part of body with black rear body. Green scale edges and thick lips. Solitary and feeds on benthic invertebrates. Shy and usually wary of divers.

Cheeklined Splendour Wrasse *Oxycheilinus digramma*
Size to 30 cm (12 in)
Variable body colouration ranging from green to pink and red. Distinctive diagonal lines on lower gill cover. Solitary and often inquisitive.

Bluestreak Cleaner Wrasse *Labroides dimidiatus*
Size to 11 cm (4¼ in)
White head and body becoming blue towards the tail with wide black stripe running the length of the body. Solitary or in pairs at cleaning stations. The most common cleaner wrasse on Seychelles reefs.

Goldbar Wrasse *Thalassoma hebraicum*
Size to 23 cm (9 in)
Orange to pink head with striking blue markings. Wide gold bar behind the pectoral fin, yellow/green body turning to blue and yellow edge to the tail.

Surge Wrasse *Thalassoma purpureum*
Size to 40 cm (16 in)
Blue to green with vivid pink/purple markings on the head. Pair of red stripes along the length of the body. As name suggests, common in the surge zone.

Greenthroat Parrotfish *Scarus prasiognathos*
Size to 70 cm (28 in)
Terminal Phase: dark blue-green with orange upper area on the head and turquoise band across the snout.

Parrotfish (Scaridae)

Blue-barred Parrotfish *Scarus ghobban*
Size to 60 cm (24 in)
Initial Phase: orange to pink body with blue spots, sometimes forming bars. Forms groups near sandy areas.

Bumphead Parrotfish *Bolbometopon muricatum*
Size to 130 cm (51 in)
Green body with pronounced hump on the forehead. Feeds on coral and algae. Typically in schools, though large groups are now very rare.

Triggerfish (Balistidae)

Steephead Parrotfish *Chlorurus strongylocephalus*
Size to 70 cm (28 in)
Terminal Phase: greenish-blue with pink scale margins. Steep forehead and yellow area on the cheek.

Orange-striped Triggerfish *Balistapus undulatus*
Size to 30 cm (12 in)
A frequently encountered triggerfish, dark green to brown with diagonal orange bands and a black spot on the base of the tail. Solitary and feeds on a variety of invertebrates.

Titan Triggerfish   *Balistoides viridescens*
Size to 60 cm (24 in)
Dark body with crosshatch pattern and yellow cheek patch. Usually solitary, this large triggerfish can be aggressive when guarding its nest.

Filefish (Monacanthidae)

Longnose Filefish   *Oxymonacanthus longirostris*
Size to 9 cm (3½ in)
Blue-green body with numerous orange spots. Found in pairs or small groups. Feeds exclusively on Acropora corals and is common on reefs where this coral is abundant.

Porcupinefish (Diodontidae)

Picasso Triggerfish   *Rhinecanthus aculeatus*
Size to 25 cm (10 in)
White-cream body with black eye bar and a yellow band from the snout. Black patch on body with diagonal bands. Very common in shallow water above seagrass and coral rubble.

Porcupinefish   *Diodon hystrix*
Size to 70 cm (28 in)
Grey to tan with white underside and numerous small black spots on head and dorsal surface of body. Covered in short spines. When threatened will inflate to become ball shaped.

Flagtail Triggerfish   *Sufflamen chrysopterus*
Size to 30 cm (12 in)
Grey to dark brown with orange bar behind the eye. Orange-brown tail with white edges. Common on patchy reefs with scattered coral.

Black-blotched Porcupinefish   *Diodon liturosus*
Size to 50 cm (20 in)
Beige body with dark blotches and pale underbelly. Large eyes and protruding mouth. Solitary, often hiding under ledges during the day. Similar appearance to pufferfish but the body is covered in short spines.

Pufferfish (Tetraodontidae)

Black-saddled Toby *Canthigaster valentini*
Size to 10 cm (4 in)
Small puffer species. White body with gold spots and four dark saddles. Solitary or forms small groups. Very common on shallow reefs within Seychelles.

Map Puffer *Arothon mappa*
Size to 65 cm (26 in)
White to grey body with black, maze-like markings. Uncommon and solitary. Feeds on sponges and benthic invertebrates.

Cowfish and boxfish (Ostraciidae)

Thornback Cowfish *Lactoria fornasini*
Size to 5 cm (6 in)
Tan undercolour with a network of bright blue markings covering the head and body. Distinctive pair of horns above the eyes and a second pair at the rear of the body. A solitary thorn located in the middle of the back.

Guineafowl Puffer *Arothon meleagris*
Size to 50 cm (20 in)
Two different colour forms: black head and body covered in small white spots or yellow head and body with occasional dark spots. Feeds on branching corals.

Yellow Boxfish *Ostracion cubicus*
Size to 45 cm (18 in)
Large adults tend to be a light purple colour while younger adults have an olive/yellow colouration with white-centered dark spots on the head and body (shown above). Juveniles bright yellow with black spots on the head and body.

Star Puffer *Arothon stellatus*
Size to 100 cm (40 in)
Largest of the puffer species. White to grey with numerous black spots and blotches. Usually solitary though occasionally in pairs.

Spotted Boxfish *Ostracion meleagris*
Size to 18 cm (7 in)
Males have a blue head/body with orange spots and a black back with white spots (shown above). Females are uniformly dark brown/black with white spots. Feeds on benthic invertebrates.

Freckled Hawkfish *Paracirrhites forsteri*
Size to 22 cm (8¾ in)
Variable colouration but often brown becoming yellow towards the tail. Numerous small dark spots on the pale head. Solitary, commonly perches on coral heads.

Hawkfish (Cirrhitidae)

Goatfish (Mullidae)

Pixy Hawkfish *Cirrhitichthys oxycephalus*
Size to 9 cm (3½ in)
Red-brown blotches cover a white undercolour. Typically hides among the branches of hard corals or at their base. Found to 40 m (130 ft).

Yellowstripe Goatfish *Mulloidichthys flavolineatus*
Size to 40 cm (16 in)
White to silver with pale yellow stripes running along the body. Black blotch below first dorsal fin, which can be 'turned off' at will.

Arceye Hawkfish *Paracirrhites arcatus*
Size to 14 cm (5½ in)
Orange to pink body with bright orange arc behind the eye and three orange dashes on the edge of the gill cover. White stripe running along the side of the body to the tail. Perches on a variety of corals.

Yellowfin Goatfish *Mulloidichthys vanicolensis*
Size to 38 cm (15 in)
White with yellow back and fins, and a yellow stripe running from the eye to the tail base. Pink to red eye rim. Forms large stationary aggregations during the day.

Dash-dot Goatfish *Parupeneus barberinus*
Size to 50 cm (20 in)
White with black stripe extending from the snout to below the second dorsal fin, occasionally yellow area above the stripe. Black dot at the base of the tail. Solitary or in small groups, often observed foraging in sandy substrate.

Finstripe Goatfish *Upeneus taeniopterus*
Size to 30 cm (12 in)
Cream body with two brown lateral body stripes. Numerous dark stripes along the caudal lobes. Forms loose aggregations.

Soldierfish and squirrelfish (Holocentridae)

Cardinal Goatfish *Parupeneus ciliatus*
Size to 38 cm (15 in)
Light red to yellow with a pair of white bands extending from in front of the eye to the second dorsal fin. Found in seagrass beds, sand, rubble and coral reef areas.

Blotcheye Soldierfish *Myripristis murdjan*
Size to 27 cm (10½ in)
Red to silver with dark scale margins. Red spiny dorsal fin and dark margin to the operculum. Solitary and in large aggregations.

Longbarbel Goatfish *Parupeneus macronema*
Size to 30 cm (12 in)
White with pink top half of the body. Black stripe from eye to beneath second dorsal fin and black spot at the base of tail. Black stripe running along the base of second dorsal fin.

Seychelles Squirrelfish *Sargocentron seychellense*
Size to 27 cm (10½ in)
Silver with thin red stripes. Spines of dorsal fin orange tipped. Common on shallow reefs, often found hiding under ledges and in amongst corals.

Sabre Squirrelfish   *Sargocentron spiniferum*
Size to 45 cm (18 in)
Red deep body shape with yellow hue to the fins. Large, distinctive, opercular spine. Solitary, often hiding under ledges during daylight hours.

Bigeyes (Priacanthidae)

Crescent Tail Bigeye   *Priacanthus hamrur*
Size to 40 cm (16 in)
Variable colour changing from red to silver and occasionally with red bars. Nocturnal, hovers under ledges or coral during the day. Often forms large groups.

Cardinalfish (Apogonidae)

Tiger Cardinalfish   *Cheilodipterus macrodon*
Size to 20 cm (8 in)
White undercolour with numerous brown stripes running the length of the body to white tail base. Found under ledges. Males incubate egg masses inside their mouths.

Sweepers (Pempheridae)

Copper Sweeper   *Pempheris oualensis*
Size to 20 cm (8 in)
Copper-brown body with black tip to the dorsal fin and a black spot at the base of the pectoral fin. Forms aggregations under ledges and coral overhangs.

Snappers (Lutjanidae)

Mangrove Jack   *Lutjanus argentimaculatus*
Size to 120 cm (47 in)
Grey to copper colour, with reddish fins. Solitary or in small aggregations. Found on both carbonate and granitic reefs as well as in mangroves.

Bengal Snapper   *Lutjanus bengalensis*
Size to 21 cm (8¼ in)
Similar to *L. kasmira* in appearance but lacks any markings on the underside. A common species often forming mixed aggregations on offshore reefs.

Red Snapper *Lutjanus bohar*
Size to 80 cm (32 in)
Silver to red with stocky body and groove beneath the eye. Juveniles have two white spots on their side. Solitary or in schools. Feeds on fish, crustaceans and cephalopods.

Bigeye Snapper *Lutjanus lutjanus*
Size to 30 cm (12 in)
One of the most common snappers within the inner islands. Silvery with yellow lateral stripe and yellow tail. Forms large aggregations at offshore sites and on wrecks.

Paddletail Snapper *Lutjanus gibbus*
Size to 50 cm (20 in)
Grey to red with humped back and distinctive rounded lobes to the tail. Orange/red colouration to edge of gill cover and base of pectoral fin, with orange/red fins. Solitary or forms large schools. Feeds on benthic fish and invertebrates.

Onespot Snapper *Lutjanus monostigma*
Size to 55 cm (22 in)
Silver to reddish body with yellow fins. Sometimes has an elongated dark spot towards the rear of the body. Solitary or forms small aggregations.

Bluelined Snapper *Lutjanus kasmira*
Size to 35 cm (14 in)
White belly with several faint lines, yellow upper body with four blue stripes. Aggregates in large schools, particularly on offshore reefs.

Black Snapper *Macolor niger*
Size to 60 cm (24 in)
Dark grey to black with elongated pectoral fins. Large eyes with a gold rim. Adults feed on zooplankton and form large schools high in water column. Juveniles have a distinctive black-and-white blotch pattern.

Red Emperor Snapper *Lutjanus sebae*
Size to 80 cm (32 in)
Red or pink body as adult, juveniles and sub adults have paler body with three distinctive dark bands. Locally known as 'Bourzwa', it is a commercially important fish usually found on deeper reefs. Feeds on small fish and benthic crustaceans.

Sweetlips (Haemulidae)

Gibbus Sweetlips *Plectorhinchus gibbosus*
Size to 75 cm (30 in)
Grey body with dark head and fins and occasional dark bar on back. Small juveniles are entirely brown and may rest on their sides to mimic a leaf.

Silver Sweetlips *Diagramma pictum*
Size to 90 cm (36 in)
Silver/grey body, juveniles and small adults with orange spots. Solitary or in small groups, usually found close to the substrate.

Spotted Sweetlips *Plectorhinchus picus*
Size to 80 cm (32 in)
White body with black spots covering the head and upper part of the body. Solitary, usually found under ledges or in caves.

Oriental Sweetlips *Plectorhinchus vittatus*
Size to 86 cm (34 in)
White with black stripes, yellow fins and lips. Usually solitary but occasionally form small, tightly packed schools. Juveniles move with an exaggerated side-to-side motion.

Groupers (Serranidae)

Slender Grouper *Anyperodon leucogrammicus*
Size to 52 cm (20½ in)
Slender gold body covered with orange/red spots. A solitary predator of small fish, common on Seychelles reefs.

Redmouth Grouper   *Aethaloperca rogaa*
Size to 60 cm (24 in)
A dark brown or black, deep-bodied grouper, the inside of the mouth is red. Solitary, usually found near caves or coral heads where they feed on small schooling fish.

Whitespotted Grouper   *Epinephelus caeruleopunctatus*
Size to 70 cm (28 in)
Dark grey body with white spots and blotches. Solitary with juveniles preferring shallow waters. Usually found under ledges or near coral.

Peacock Grouper   *Cephalopholis argus*
Size to 40 cm (16 in)
Brown body covered in blue spots, with blue fins and tail. Can change body colour to become lighter or darker. Usually solitary but can form small groups. Sometimes observed nuclear hunting with other fish.

Blacktip Grouper   *Epinephelus fasciatus*
Size to 40 cm (16 in)
Highly variable colouration ranging from white body with red head to red/brown body with dark bars. Black tips to dorsal spines. A common grouper on Seychelles reefs although larger individuals are rarely seen.

Coral Hind   *Cephalopholis miniata*
Size to 41 cm (16½ in)
Orange to red body with bright blue spots. Solitary, though several individuals will occupy the same area of reef. Prefers structurally complex reefs with large coral colonies.

Honeycomb Grouper   *Epinephelus merra*
Size to 30 cm (12 in)
Hexagonal beige/brown spots on a white undercolour. Usually found in shallow reef environments.

Camouflage Grouper *Epinephelus polyphekadion*
Size to 75 cm (30 in)
Pale brown with dark blotches on upper half of body and dark saddle on tail base. Lower half of body displays dense honeycomb pattern. Solitary, feeds on crustaceans and fish. Usually found in coral-rich areas near crevices and overhangs.

African Coral Cod *Plectropomus punctatus*
Size to 96 cm (38 in)
Slender, dark-bodied grouper with blue margins to fins. Juveniles display pale 'morse code' pattern on body. Solitary or in small groups, feeds on fish.

Foursaddle Grouper *Epinephelus spilotoceps*
Size to 31 cm (12¼ in)
Various shades of brown with tightly packed, polygon-shaped spots. Four dark saddles on the back. Solitary, often out in the open resting on the substrate.

Scale-fin Anthias *Pseudanthias squamipinnis*
Size to 5 cm (2 in)
Female is orange with purple stripe running from eye to pectoral fin. Male red/purple with yellow scales on the body, a pink blotch on pectoral fin and a long dorsal spine. Form plankton-feeding aggregations, with females greatly outnumbering haremic males.

Emperors (Lethrinidae)

Saddleback Grouper *Plectropomus laevis*
Size to 125 cm (49 in)
White elongated body with four black saddles, yellow nape and fins. Also found in a grey to brown colour variation. Feeds on a variety of reef fish. Usually wary and difficult to approach.

Yellow Spot Emperor *Gnathodentex aurolineatus*
Size to 30 cm (12 in)
Silver with gold stripes along the body. Yellow blotch below rear dorsal fin. Solitary or in large schools near coral during the day. Feeds on benthic invertebrates at night.

Thumbprint Emperor *Lethrinus harak*
Size to 50 cm (20 in)
Pale grey with single dark spot on side of body, sometimes surrounded by orange ring. Found in seagrass beds and shallow sand/rubble areas, where it feeds on benthic invertebrates.

Bigeye Bream *Monotaxis grandoculis*
Size to 60 cm (24 in)
Dark body with pale underside. Yellow tint on head and black spot at the base of the pectoral fin. Sub-adults have white bars and a yellow tail. Usually found hovering motionless in the water column.

Threadfin Breams (Nemipteridae)

Orange-stripe Emperor *Lethrinus obsoletus*
Size to 50 cm (20 in)
Pale grey to silver with orange stripe from the pectoral fin to the base of the tail. Can quickly change colour to mottled pattern. Common over seagrass beds and rubble.

Bridled Monocle Bream *Scolopsis frenatus*
Size to 26 cm (10¼ in)
Upper body blue to brown in colour and lower body white. A yellow stripe runs through the upper part of the eye to behind the dorsal fin. Solitary or in groups, close above the substrate. Feeds on benthic invertebrates.

Fusiliers (Caesionidae)

Red Ear Emperor *Lethrinus rubrioperculatus*
Size to 50 cm (20 in)
Brown to silver with pale mottled bars and stripes on lower part of body. Torpedo-shaped body. Red spot on edge of gill cover. Prefers sand and rubble areas.

Scissortail Fusilier *Caesio caerulaurea*
Size to 35 cm (14 in)
Silver to blue with bright yellow stripe along the body and dark streak on tail lobes. Often forms large, mixed, mid-water aggregations with other fusilier species.

Blue and Yellow Fusilier *Caesio teres*
Size to 35 cm (14 in)
Similar in appearance to *C. xanthonota* with silver to blue body, but yellow extends only from the back to the tail. Forms aggregations often mixing with other fusilier species.

Bluestreak Fusilier *Pterocaesio tile*
Size to 25 cm (10 in)
Blue iridescent band along the length of the body. Underside silvery blue to red. The only member of the genus *Pterocaesio* with dark borders to the tail. Forms large aggregations. Planktivore.

Monos (Monodactylidae)

Yellowback Fusilier *Caesio xanthonota*
Size to 35 cm (14 in)
Silver to blue body. Tail, top of head and back are bright yellow. Forms large aggregations, often associated with other fusilier species. More common during the south-east monsoon when plankton is plentiful.

Diamondfish *Monodactylus argenteus*
Size to 27 cm (10½ in)
Laterally compressed, silver body with yellow triangular dorsal and anal fins. Forms large schools close to the granite reefs and brackish water. A very common species within the inner islands.

Queenfish (Scomberoididae)

Twinstripe Fusilier *Pterocaesio marri*
Size to 35 cm (14 in)
Silvery blue to green with pair of narrow yellow stripes above the lateral line. Dark tips to the tail. Forms large mixed aggregations in water column.

Double-spotted Queenfish *Scomberoides lysan*
Size to 77 cm (30 in)
Silver body with dark leading edge to dorsal and anal fins. Three dark spots on the side of the body. Juveniles often found in shallow water.

Jacks (Carangidae)

Blue-fin Trevally   *Caranx melampygus*
Size to 100 cm (40 in)
Silvery blue body with numerous blue spots and blue fins. Solitary or forms schools, which are often observed hunting above the reef. A common jack species within the inner islands.

Bigeye Trevally   *Caranx sexfasciatus*
Size to 100 cm (40 in)
Completely silver body with black spot on the upper part of the gill cover and white tip to the rear dorsal fin. Forms large schools and will often approach divers closely.

Golden Trevally   *Gnathanodon speciosus*
Size to 120 cm (47 in)
Silvery yellow body with black patches or bars. Juveniles bright yellow to gold with distinctive black bars, often found accompanying other large pelagic fishes.

Snubnose Pompano   *Trachinotus blochii*
Size to 110 cm (44 in)
Oval silver body with elongated yellow pectoral and anal fins, blunt snout. Solitary or forms schools. Inquisitive and will often approach divers.

Batfish (Ephippididae)

Orbicular Batfish   *Platax orbicularis*
Size to 50 cm (20 in)
Similar to *P. teira* but lacks the black blotch in front of the anal fin. Solitary or in small groups, occasionally in large aggregations. Curious and will approach divers.

Teira Batfish   *Platax teira*
Size to 60 cm (24 in)
Triangular silver body with dark bar through the eye and a second before the dorsal fin. Black blotch in front of anal fin. Solitary or in small groups.

Barracudas (Sphyraenidae)

Great Barracuda   *Sphyraena barracuda*
Size to 180 cm (71 in)
Long silvery body with scattered dark blotches and dark tail. Large lower jaw with numerous pointed teeth. Pelagic species and feeds on other fish. Curious and will approach closely.

Sawtooth Barracuda   *Sphyraena putnamiae*
Size to 90 cm (36 in)
Silver with numerous chevrons running along the length of the body. Forms large schools adjacent to reefs. Inquisitive and will often approach divers.

Cornetfish (Fistulariidae)

Cornetfish   *Fistularia commersonii*
Size to 150 cm (59 in)
Sliver to blue, thin, elongated body. Has the ability to change colour to display prominent banding. Solitary or in schools, feeds on small fish and crustaceans. Can be differentiated from *A. chinensis* by a whip-like tail filament.

Blackfin Barracuda   *Sphyraena qenie*
Size to 120 cm (47 in)
Silvery elongated body with dark tail. Numerous chevron markings along the length of the body. Forms large schools, commonly found at offshore dive sites.

Trumpetfish (Aulostomidae)

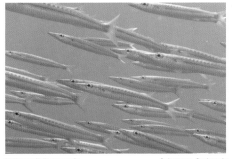

Yellowtail Barracuda   *Sphyraena flavicauda*
Size to 50 cm (20 in)
Smaller than other barracuda species. Silver body with yellow tail and narrow pair of brown stripes running along the body. Forms large schools above the reef.

Trumpetfish   *Aulostomus chinensis*
Size to 80 cm (32 in)
Can be bright yellow or silver, both colour variations are relatively common. Often observed shadow hunting with other fish, such as grouper, or drifting head down in an attempt to ambush prey.

Blennies (Blenniidae)

Nalolo Blenny   *Ecsenius nalolo*
Size to 6.5 cm (2½ in)
Dusky body with white spots and pink area on top of the head between
the eyes. Usually found on coral or rubble substrate.

Bluestriped Fangblenny   *Plagiotremus tapeinosoma*
Size to 12 cm (4¾ in)
Orange with pair of bright blue stripes running the length of the body.
Juveniles mimic cleaner wrasse. Feeds on scales and skin of other fish
and on occasion may bite if approached closely.

Gobies (Gobiidae)

Pinkeye Goby   *Bryaninops natans*
Size to 2.5 cm (1 in)
Translucent body with yellow belly and bright pink eye. Usually found
in groups hovering above Acropora corals, occasionally resting on
the coral tips.

Wire Coral Goby   *Bryaninops yongei*
Size to 3.5 cm (1⅜ in)
Body is translucent with red bars and eye ring. Found only on the Wire
Coral *Cirripathes anguina*. Usually solitary but occasionally can be
found in small groups on an individual coral.

Striped Pygmygoby   *Eviota sebreei*
Size to 2.5 cm (1 in)
Transparent body with a dark mid line and white dashes on top of the
body. Usually found in small groups resting on top of boulder corals,
such as Porites.

Lemon Goby   *Gobiodon citrinus*
Size to 6 cm (2½ in)
Variable in colour, though the yellow form is most common within the
inner islands. All variants possess a double blue bar through the eye
and second double bar further back on the head. Lives among the
branches of Acropora corals.

Mullet (Mugilidae)

Fringe lip mullet *Crenimugil crenilabis*
Size to 40 cm (16 in)
Silvery body with black spot on upper pectoral fin base and wide upper lip. Forms schools in shallow water and can be seen feeding in the sand.

Scorpionfish, Stonefish and Lionfish (Scorpaenidae)

Leaf Scorpionfish *Taenianotus.triacanthus*
Size to 10 cm (4 in)
Compressed flat body with tall dorsal fin. Highly variable colouration with yellow, white and brown specimens all common within the inner islands. Sways from side to side, mimicking a piece of debris or leaf.

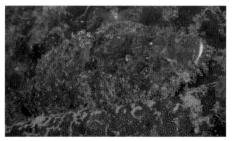

Tassled Scorpionfish *Scorpaenopsis oxycephala*
Size to 35 cm (14 in)
Variable colour, often blending in with the substrate it is resting on. Humped snout and numerous tassels along the lower edge of the head. Ambush predator.

Devil Scorpionfish *Scorpaenopsis diabolus*
Size to 28 cm (11 in)
Highly variable colouration, usually blending in with the substrate. Distinctive humped back and orange, yellow and black colour to the inside of the pectoral fins. Solitary or in pairs, often on seagrass or rubble.

Indian Ocean Walkman *Inimicus filamentosus*
Size to 22 cm (8¾ in)
Large upturned mouth and eyes set on top of the head. Pronounced dorsal spines and fan-like pectoral fins, which it uses for walking across substrate. Usually found on sand or rubble, sometimes burying itself with only the eyes visible.

Indian Lionfish *Pterois muricata*
Size to 38 cm (15 in)
White underside with red-brown to black bands. Long, narrow pectoral and dorsal fin rays. Solitary or forms groups which can be easily approached.

Stonefish   *Synanceia verrucosa*
Size to 35 cm (14 in)
Colour variable and often mottled, difficult to pick out against surroundings. Numerous skin flaps break up its outline. Eyes widely spaced and separated by a deep depression. Large upturned mouth. A highly venomous species; wounds caused by spines can be fatal.

Eeltail Catfish (Plotosidae)

Striped Eel Catfish   *Plotosus lineatus*
Size to 32 cm (12½ in)
Dark brown with white underside and pair of white stripes along the body. Distinctive barbels around the mouth. Juveniles often school together in tightly packed balls of hundreds of fish.

Lizardfish (Synodontidae)

Reef Lizardfish   *Synodus variegatus*
Size to 24 cm (9½ in)
Brown, red or grey with dark saddles along the body. Solitary or in pairs, remains motionless on the substrate.

Shrimpfish (Centriscidae)

Razorfish   *Aeoliscus strigatus*
Size to 5 cm (6 in)
Silver flattened body with dark stripe along lateral line. Forms schools that swim in a head-down position above the reef.

Dartfish (Microdesmidae)

Fire Dartfish   *Nemateleotris magnifica*
Size to 7 cm (2¾ in)
Front of body is white, turning to orange red near the rear. Elongated first dorsal fin. Often found in pairs, hovering above coral rubble at the edge of the reef. If disturbed will disappear into its burrow.

Sandperch (Pinguipedidae)

Redspotted Sandperch   *Parapercis schauinslandii*
Size to 18 cm (7 in)
Initial portion of dorsal fin black with red edge, followed by row of black spots. Pale with series of dark bars on body. As the name suggests, usually found perching on the sandy substrate.

Ghost Pipefish (Solenostomidae)

Pipefish (Syngnathidae)

Robust Ghost Pipefish *Solenostomus cyanopterus*
Size to 16 cm (6¼ in)
Variable colour including red, yellow and brown. Long narrow body with broad ventral and tail fins. Usually solitary or in pairs. Mimics seagrass fronds swaying in the current.

Yellow-red Pipefish *Corythoichthys* sp.
Size to 12 cm (4¾ in)
Cream to yellow with narrow stripes along body and black stripes on the head. Numerous faint bands encircle the body. Solitary or in small groups, usually on rubble substrate.

Eels

Order Anguilliformes

Eels do not have pectoral or ventral fins like other fish. Their dorsal, tail and anal fins form one continuous fin that starts behind the head and extends the length of the body. Snake eels have an even less developed fin. Moray eels need to move water over their gills to breathe and they do this by opening and closing their mouths, a behaviour which is often misinterpreted as threatening. Eels are usually seen with their head poking out of recesses in the reef, but can also be seen swimming in the open in a side-to-side motion.

Moray Eels (Muraenidae)

Zebra Moray *Gymnomuraena zebra*
Size to 150 cm (59 in)
Dark brown body with thin white bands. Solitary and feeds mainly on crabs. Occasionally seen out in the open.

Yellow-edged Moray *Gymnothorax flavimarginatus*
Size to 240 cm (95 in)
A large moray eel, yellow-brown in colour with orange iris. Solitary and inquisitive.

Giant Moray *Gymnothorax javanicus*
Size to 300 cm (118 in)
Brown with numerous brown or black spots running the length of the body. Solitary and feeds mainly on fish and crustaceans.

Whitemouth Moray *Gymnothorax meleagris*
Size to 120 cm (47 in)
Dark brown with numerous white spots. Inside of the mouth is white. A common moray eel within the inner islands.

Banded Snake Eel   *Myrichthys colubrinus*
Size to 90 cm (36 in)
White with black bars. Inhabits sandy areas in shallow water, often seen out in the open. Solitary.

Geometric Moray   *Gymnothorax grisea*
Size to 65 cm (26 in)
Grey body with black spots on the head. Solitary or in small aggregations. The most common moray eel within the inner islands.

Sharks and Rays

Class Chondrichthyes
Sharks are found in various forms and sizes, but all are categorized by having a cartilaginous skeleton and between five and seven gill slits. Some species need to keep moving to survive while others are able to rest on the bottom, opening and closing their mouths to force water over their gills. While numerous shark species are found within Seychelles waters, most do not venture close to the shore and are unlikely to be encountered by divers and snorkellers.

Rays are close relatives of sharks but have flattened bodies and gills on their underside. Many species of ray spend most of their life on the substrate, while some, like the Mobula Rays, remain high in the water column. Rays tend to be harmless, though care should be taken when walking in shallow water as some species of stingray have barbs that are capable of inflicting painful wounds if trodden on.

Requiem Sharks (Carcharhinidae)

Grey Reef Shark   *Carcharhinus amblyrhynchos*
Size to 230 cm (91 in)
Grey with white underside and black tail margin. Often has white trailing margin to the top of the dorsal fin. Solitary or in schools. Known to aggregate at specific sites during certain times of the year.

Blacktip Reef Shark   *Carcharhinus melanopterus*
Size to 180 cm (71 in)
Yellowish/brown to grey with white undersides and distinctive black tips to fins. Solitary or in groups, usually in very shallow water. Uncommon around the inner granitic islands.

Lemon Shark *Negaprion acutidens*
Size to 310 cm (122 in)
Yellowish-brown with pale underside and lacking any markings. Pair of similar sized dorsal fins. Juveniles often found in shallow water and mangroves.

Whitetip Reef Shark *Triaenodon obesus*
Size to 210 cm (83 in)
Grey body with white tips to dorsal fin and tail. Often rests on the bottom, either out in the open or in caves. The most common shark observed within the inner islands.

Nurse Sharks (Ginglymostomatidae)

Nurse Shark *Nebrius ferrugineus*
Size to 320 cm (126 in)
Light brown or grey and lacking markings. Small mouth with pair of nasal barbels. Dorsal fins set back towards the tail. Often found resting under ledges. Feeds on small fish, crustaceans and cephalopods.

Whale Sharks (Rhincodontidae)

Whale Shark *Rhincodon typus*
Size to 12 m (40 ft)
Dark upper body with numerous white spots and bars and white underside. Feeds on zooplankton and is often accompanied by numerous pilot fish and remoras. Aggregates near shore during the months of August to October when the plankton levels are high.

Whiptail Stingrays (Dasyatidae)

Feathertail Ray   *Pastinachus ater*
Size to 180 cm (71 in)
Beige to brown. Diamond-shaped pectoral fins, with distinctive fleshy fold at the end of the tail. Solitary or forms aggregations often in shallow water.

Marbled Ray   *Taeniura meyeni*
Size to 180 cm (71 in)
Dark grey with black blotches. Smaller individuals rest under coral outcrops and ledges. Larger individuals out in the open, often inquisitive and will approach closely.

Thorny Ray   *Urogymnus asperrimus*
Size to 100 cm (40 in)
Humped grey body covered with numerous spines. Has a short tail. Often buried in the sand, frequently found in shallow water.

Manta and Devil Rays (Mobulidae)

Manta Ray   *Manta alfredi*
Size to 500 cm (200 in)
Grey to black dorsal surface sometimes with pale or dark areas, and white underside. Large triangular wings with pair of head flaps. Distinguished from Devil Rays by their unique spot pattern on their underside. Seasonal visitors to the granitic inner islands.

Devil Ray   *Mobula kuhlii*
Size to 120 cm (47 in)
Tan to dark brown with white underside. White-tipped dorsal fin. Swims in mid-water, often in large schools.

Eagle Rays (Myliobatidae)

Spotted Eagle Ray   *Aetobatus ocellatus*
Size to 300 cm (118 in)
Grey to black dorsal surface with numerous white spots and white underside. Solitary or in groups. Those found in Seychelles rarely attain more than 100 cm (40 in) in size.

Sea Turtles

Class Reptilia
Family Cheloniidae
A marine reptile, sea turtles are one of the oldest living species in the world. There are five recorded species of turtle in Seychelles but only Green and Hawksbill Turtles are frequently encountered and nest on the beaches of Seychelles.

Green Turtles are found throughout tropical and subtropical seas around the world. The name Green Turtle describes the layer of fat beneath the carapace rather than the colour of the animal. Listed on the IUCN Red List as 'Endangered'. While they are common around the outer islands, and in particular Aldabra Atoll, much lower numbers are thought to nest within the inner islands. Green Turtles feed primarily on seagrass and are often encountered on shallow seagrass beds as well as on coral reefs.

Hawksbill Turtles are found throughout the tropics, though years of being hunted for their carapace have led to their current listing on the IUCN Red List as 'Critically Endangered'. Seychelles is fortunate in being one of a handful of locations where Hawksbill Turtles nest during daylight hours, meaning it is possible to observe nesting activity on certain undisturbed beaches. Closely associated with coral reefs where they feed on sponges, Hawksbills are the most common turtle species encountered when snorkelling or diving around the islands.

Sea Turtles (Cheloniidae)

Green Turtle *Chelonia mydas*
Size to 140 cm (55 in)
A large turtle species, their carapace is teardrop shaped and the head has a blunt beak.

Hawksbill Turtle *Eretmochelys imbricata*
Size to 100 cm (40 in)
Has a characteristic hawk-like beak and an often-serrated trailing edge to their carapace. The most common turtle species encountered in the inner islands.

Glossary

Appendage A projecting part of an invertebrate or other organism with a distinct appearance or function.

Benthos The plants and animals found on the bottom of the sea or any other body of water.

Carapace The hard upper shell of a turtle or crustacean.

Cerata Fleshy structures on the dorsal side of some nudibranchs.

Coral bleaching A breakdown in the symbiotic relationship between coral polyps and zooxanthellae leading to the expulsion of the algae and a loss of pigmentation in the coral. Coral bleaching is caused by a number of stressors including pollution, sedimentation and disease, but is most commonly a result of prolonged, elevated sea temperatures.

Corallite The cup-like, calcareous skeleton of a single coral polyp.

Corallivore An animal that feeds on coral polyps.

Decompression Sickness (DCS) Also known as 'the bends', DCS occurs when there is a sudden drop in the surrounding pressure of the body. Nitrogen gas bubbles form in the blood and tissues, and block the flow of blood.

Detritivore An animal that feeds on detritus.

Diurnal (of animals) most active during the day.

Dorsal Of, on, or relating to the upper side or back of an animal or plant.

El Niño An irregularly occurring and complex series of climatic changes affecting the equatorial Pacific region and beyond every few years, characterized by the appearance of unusually warm, nutrient-poor water off northern Peru and Ecuador.

Ecological niche A position or role occupied by an organism within its community and environment.

Ecosystem A biological community of interacting organisms and their physical environment.

Endemic Native to or restricted to a certain country or area.

Exclusive Economic Zone (EEZ) An area of coastal water and seabed within a certain distance of a country's coastline to which the country claims exclusive rights for fishing, exploration and additional economic activities.

Genus A grouping of organisms having common characteristics distinct from those of other such groupings. It is a taxonomic category that ranks above Species and below Family.

Gondwana A vast continental area believed to have existed in the southern hemisphere and to have resulted from the break-up of the supercontinent of Pangaea in Mesozoic times (c.200 million years ago). It comprised the present Arabia, Africa, South America, Antarctica, Australia, New Zealand and the peninsula of India.

Invertebrate Any animal lacking a backbone or spinal column.

Invertivore An animal that feeds on invertebrates.

IUCN Red List A comprehensive inventory of the global conservation status of plant and animal species. It uses a set of criteria to evaluate the extinction risk of thousands of species and subspecies.

Mantle (of Mollusca) a fold of skin located on the dorsal surface of the animal.

NGO Non-Governmental Organization.

Nocturnal (of animals) most active at night.

Nuclear hunting A type of association where two or more species forage together.

Operculum A hard bony flap that covers and protects a fish's gills.

Papillae Small rounded protuberances on a part or organ of the body.

Pelagic (of fish) inhabits the upper water column of the sea.

Photosynthesis The process by which plants and other organisms use sunlight to synthesize foods from carbon dioxide and water.

Piscivore An animal that feeds on fish.

Planktivore An animal that feeds on plankton.

Rhinophores A pair of club-shaped structures located on the head of nudibranchs. They are sensory organs that are used for taste and smell.

Sessile An immobile organism, fixed in one place.

Spicule A small needle or spine.

Substrate An underlying layer or surface on which an organism grows or to which it is attached.

Symbiosis A close association of two different species that live together, which may be of mutual benefit to each other.

Tailing behaviour (of nudibranchs) when one animal follows another animal's trail.

Taxon (pl. taxa) A taxonomic group of any rank, e.g. Species, Family, Class.

The bends See 'Decompression Sickness'

Zooplankton Plankton that consists of small animals (as opposed to phytoplankton that is formed of plants).

Zooxanthellae Microscopic algae that live symbiotically in reef-building corals.

Further reading and useful websites

Books

Allen, G., Steene, R., Humann, P. and Deloach, N. 2003. *Reef Fish Identification, Tropical Pacific*. New World Publications, Inc, Jacksonville, USA

Bergbauer, M. & Kirschner, M. 2014. *Diving and Snorkelling Guide to Tropical Marine Life of the Indo-Pacific Region*. John Beaufoy Publishing, Oxford, UK

Bergbauer, M. & Kirschner, M. 2014. *Reef Fishes of the Indo-Pacific*. John Beaufoy Publishing, Oxford, UK

Debelius, H. 1993. *Indian Ocean – Tropical Fish Guide*. Aquaprint Verlags, Neu Isenberg, Germany

Debelius, H. 1999. *Indian Ocean Reef Guide*. IKAN Unterwasser Archiv, Frankfurt

Humann, P. & Deloach, N. 2010. *Reef Creature Identification, Tropical Pacific*. New World Publications, Inc, Jacksonville, USA

Jarrett, A.G. 2000. *Marine Shells of Seychelles*. Carole Green Publishing, Cambridge, UK

Lieske, E. & Meyers, R. 1994. *Coral Reef Fishes: Caribbean, Indian Ocean and Pacific Ocean*. Collins Pocket Guide. Harper Collins, London, UK

Hill, M. & Currie, D. 2007. *Wildlife of Seychelles*. Collins Traveller's Guide. Harper Collins, London

Websites

Dive Centres

Big Blue Divers - www.bigbluedivers.net
Blue Sea Divers - blueseadivers.com
Dive Resort Seychelles - www.scubadiveseychelles.com
Eco-center - eco-center.jimdo.com
Hawksbill Dive Center – www.hawksbilldivecenter.com
Ocean Dream Divers - www.oceandreamdivers.eu/index.html
Octopus Diver - www.octopusdiver.com
Trek Divers – www.trekdivers.com
Underwater Centre - www.diveseychelles.com.sc
Whitetip Divers - www.whitetipdivers.com

Liveaboards

Diving Cruises Seychelles - www.diving-cruises.com
Silhouette Cruises - www.seychelles-cruises.com

NGOs & Government Departments

Global Vision International – www.gvi.co.uk
Green Islands Foundation - greenislandsfoundation.blogspot.com
Island Conservation Society - www.islandconservationseychelles.com
MarineBio Conservation Society - www.marinebio.org
Marine Conservation Society Seychelles - www.mcss.sc
Nature Seychelles - www.natureseychelles.org
Save Our Seas Foundation – www.saveourseas.com
Seychelles Islands Foundation – www.sif.sc
Seychelles National Parks Authority - www.snpa.sc
WiseOceans – www.wiseoceans.com

Marine Creature Identification

Coral Identification - coral.aims.gov.au
Fish Base - www.fishbase.org
MarineBio Conservation Society - marinebio.org
World Register of Marine Species (WoRMS) - www.marinespecies.org

Others

Archipelago Images – www.archipelagoimages.net
Dream Yacht Charters - www.dreamyachtcharter.com/
Seychelles Tourism Board - www.seychelles.travel

Acknowledgements

The authors would like to thank the many people who offered advice and support during the writing of this book.

A special thanks to David and Sharon Walton who provided guidance and encouragement from the beginning, when the idea for this book was first conceived. Their revision of the manuscript was also invaluable.

We would also like to offer our sincere gratitude to both David and Glynis Rowat of the Underwater Centre on Mahé and Florent and Hélène Le Bihan of Octopus Divers on Praslin, who both offered diving support to allow us the necessary underwater photographic time needed for this book.

Our thanks to Lindsay Sullivan and Abbie Hine of WiseOceans, who both gave up their time to review the identification section. Thanks also to John Nevill for his contribution. Your knowledge was invaluable!

To John Beaufoy and Rosemary Wilkinson of John Beaufoy Publishing, thank you for your backing of and commitment to the production of this book. We are especially grateful that you saw the vision we had for this book and were willing to take a chance on us.

We hope that this book will inspire and invoke a passion for the magnificent underwater world of Seychelles. This book is dedicated to all those individuals and organizations who have worked and continue to work tirelessly towards conserving and protecting this precious marine environment.

Author Profiles

Christophe Mason-Parker has been fascinated by the marine environment for as long as he can remember. He has worked on several conservation projects from Southeast Asia to the Caribbean and is now living in Seychelles where he runs Global Vision International's volunteer-based, marine and terrestrial conservation expeditions.

Chris is an enthusiastic underwater photographer and a dedicated advocate of marine conservation. Further examples of his photography can be found at his website www.archipelagoimages.net

Rowana holds an MSc in Biodiversity, Wildife and Ecosystem Health, sits on the board of several NGOs and is experienced in conservation communication and education. Rowana lived in Seychelles for many years and is passionate about the marine environment of this incredible country.

Index

Quick reference index for marine creature identification